THE SIGN OF LIFE

John Suggit

THE SIGN OF LIFE

Studies in the fourth gospel
and the liturgy of the church

John Suggit

ISBN 0-9583807-1-6

First published 1993
Cluster Publications
PO Box 2400
Pietermaritzburg 3200
Republic of South Africa

A project of the Pietermaritzburg
Cluster of Theological Institutions

Cover illustration: © Michael Merifield
Composition based on Byzantine mosaics; the miracle of
Cana, the multiplication of the loaves and the Christ
Pantocrator found in the Chora Church, Istanbul

Design and production: Barry D Lotz

Printed by Galvin & Sales
Cape Town
Republic of South Africa

Printing history

10 9 8 7 6 5 4 3 2 1   93 94 95 96 97 98 99

Contents

Preface

It is a rash venture to attempt to add anything to the huge corpus of literature on the fourth gospel. This slender volume is an attempt to show the intimate relationship between the written word and the proclamation of the gospel in liturgy. Though it attempts to appeal to serious students (and therefore a list of works cited is provided), it is meant especially for clergy and ministers and for those preparing for ordination, in order to help them understand how the gospel is reflected in the church's liturgy of baptism and eucharist. For this reason it should be of interest to any Christian who is concerned to devote sufficient attention to the text of the fourth gospel.

Although some knowledge of Greek would naturally be of help in understanding the New Testament, anyone who is prepared to read these pages carefully with the aid of the RSV or the NRSV should find it possible to follow the argument. Therefore Greek and Hebrew words have been transliterated and translated, and all foreign quotations are given in an English version. The translations of these, as of the scriptures (unless otherwise stated), are my own.

There are innumerable people to whom I am indebted for anything of value in the following pages. I have learnt much not only from the authors cited, but from so many others whose writings have helped me to understand the fourth gospel. If I have failed to mention them by name it is because I have so appreciated their insights that I cannot tell whether they are theirs or mine.

I am indebted too to students of St Paul's College and Rhodes University, Grahamstown, to clergy of the Church of the Province of Southern Africa, to the New Testament Society of South Africa and to many others with whom I have tried to share my ideas.

I owe gratitude to the Human Sciences Research Council for a grant to enable me to spend a term at Oxford in 1989 to complete the work, and to the Principal of Wycliffe Hall for hospitality during the period. Mr Barry Lotz of Fish Hoek has been of invaluable help in checking biblical references and generally in preparing the script for publication.

I am particularly grateful to the Archbishop of Cape Town, the Most Reverend Desmond Tutu, for his ready willingness to contribute a Foreword, especially in view of his understanding of the close relationship between liturgy and life in this troubled land of South Africa.

John Suggit
Fish Hoek
1992

Acknowledgements

The author thanks the editors of *Neotestamentica* and the *Journal of Theology for Southern Africa (JThSA)* for permission to use in slightly altered form, articles already published, as follows:

Chapter 2: *Neotestamentica* 21(2) (1987), 141-158.

The first part of Chapter 6: *Neotestamentica* 19 (1985), 64-70.

Part of Chapter 8: *JThSA* 16 (Sept 1976), 52-59 under the title "The eucharistic significance of John 20:19-29".

The financial assistance of the Institute for Research Development of the Human Sciences Research Council for the completion of this research is hereby acknowledged. Opinions expressed in this publication and conclusions arrived at are those of the author and do not necessarily represent the views of the Institute for Research Development or the Human Sciences Research Council.

Foreword

by The Most Reverend Desmond M Tutu,
Archbishop of Cape Town.

John Suggit has an enviable record of solid scholarship and in our church we look up to him. He uses his intellectual gifts for the pragmatic purpose of our edification in the real sense of building us up in the body of Christ, so that we may be more effective in our task of extending the kingdom of God in our part of God's creation.

It seems to me that John Suggit's concern may be paralleled with that of his namesake who gave us the fourth gospel. Whatever else it may be, this gospel's declared intention was that those who heard it or who read it might believe that Jesus Christ was the Son of God and in so believing might have eternal life. Its purpose is deeply soteriological. This gospel is clearly the result of a long and profound reflection on the life, death and resurrection of Jesus Christ and the significance of these events in the divine drama of our salvation.

Canon Suggit has demonstrated in a highly readable account that this gospel is one with deep layers of meaning, requiring a knowledge at the very least of the Old Testament, because it is replete with symbolism, a symbolism that makes sense in the *Sitz im Leben* of a worshipping community. Although there are in it very few direct and explicit references to the liturgical and sacramental worship of the church, there are many allusive references which would not have failed to be noticed by Christians regularly engaging in that worship. References to bread and wine, flesh and blood, to the Passover, to the bridegroom, would almost certainly ring a bell in the consciousness of many Christian worshippers, bringing to mind the eucharist, the cup and the bread of sacrifice, the Messianic banquet at the end of time.

The different levels of meaning and the diversity and richness of symbolism in the gospel are almost bewildering - as with the references to Nathanael (Jn 1:43-51), the true Israelite who comes to the true Israel who alone has seen God (from what we are told is a rabbinical but wrong definition of Israel). Because of this rich symbolism Canon Suggit calls his book *The Sign of Life*. It deals with certain key passages in the gospel to demonstrate that the signs in John point to Jesus who is himself the Sign *par excellence* as the revealer of God.

Canon Suggit has shown at least three things:

a) The centrality of worship and of the sacraments in the community for which John was writing. His gospel seems to make a great deal more sense if the dominical sacraments of baptism and eucharist and their celebration in the liturgical worship of the church are accepted as the *Sitz im Leben* of the gospel.

In the time that the church in South Africa has been in the forefront of the struggle against the viciousness of apartheid, worship has played a prominent part in upholding the people's spirits, keeping their hope burning and maintaining their confidence that God's goodness and justice will ultimately prevail. Many of us would have collapsed long ago in our battle against the principalities and powers had we not been sustained by our membership of this worldwide fellowship, the church, in which we knew someone somewhere was praying for us, and which through worship and the sacraments has been keeping us in touch with the source of all goodness and life and strength.

b) Secondly, Canon Suggit has shown persuasively that there can be no rigidity in understanding the meaning of the words of scripture which is tied irrevocably to the sacraments. We need to sit humbly before the text and allow it to speak to us as the Holy Spirit leads us to all truth. Within reasonable parameters we must be free to find that meaning which has resonance for us, but not ultimately apart from the fellowship and its tradition. The scriptures are not dead letters. They are the word of God which interacts with us. Like poems and great literature their meaning is not exhausted by what their original writers might have meant to convey.

c) Thirdly, the book has the pragmatic purpose of helping us become more effective Christians, witnessing to the love of God for his world, concerned that his life should course through the world as its lifeblood, subverting all evil, injustice, ugliness and hatred, and working for goodness and laughter and joy and peace and love and caring and compassion and sharing - all this for the kingdom of God (an unJohannine expression), and for the glory of God which was revealed supremely on the cross of Jesus Christ.

Canon Suggit's short commentary will repay being read and reread slowly and reflectively and indeed prayerfully. Though scholarly and erudite it is deeply devotional and has a way of driving you to your knees.

As his Archbishop, I am proud of John Suggit and thank God for him for this particular work and pray that it will be widely used for the edification of the church.

✝ Desmond Cape Town

Abbreviations

Books of the Bible

Old Testament

Gen	Genesis
Ex	Exodus
Lev	Leviticus
Num	Numbers
Dt	Deuteronomy
Kg	Kings (LXX Regnorum iii-iv)
Neh	Nehemiah
Ps	Psalms
Is	Isaiah
Jer	Jeremiah
Ezk	Ezekiel
Dan	Daniel
Mal	Malachi

Apocrypha

Wisdom	Wisdom of Solomon
Sir	Sirach (Ecclesiasticus)
Macc	Maccabees
Ps Sol	Psalms of Solomon

New Testament

Mk	Mark
Mt	Matthew
Lk	Luke
Jn	John
Ac	Acts
Rom	Romans
Cor	Corinthians
Gal	Galatians
Eph	Ephesians
Phil	Philippians
Col	Colossians
Th	Thessalonians
Tim	Timothy
Tit	Titus
Heb	Hebrews
Pet	Peter
1 Jn	First epistle of John
Rev	Revelation (Apocalypse)

Versions of the Bible

AV	Authorized Version
GNB	Good News Bible
LXX	Septuagint (Greek Old Testament)
NEB	New English Bible
NRSV	New Revised Standard Version
REB	Revised English Bible
RSV	Revised Standard Version

Other abbreviations

Jos	Josephus
par	parallel passages in synoptic gospels
PG	J-P Migne (ed) *Patrologia Graeca*
PL	J-P Migne (ed) *Patrologia Latina*
S	Codex Sinaiticus

All other mss cited as in Nestle-Aland[26]

The sign of life

I have never doubted the truth of signs, Adso; they
are the only things man has with which to orient
himself in the world. (William)

U Eco *The Name of the Rose* (Secker & Warburg
1983) 492

The church's eucharist

One of the most significant factors in the life of the church in
this century has been the renewed understanding of the central
position of the eucharist in its worship and life. Although this
has always been a feature of orthodox and catholic forms of
spirituality, it is now being recognized by all Christian churches.
The report of the World Council of Churches *Baptism, eucharist
and ministry* (WCC: 1982) shows the remarkable agreement
reached by theologians representing very different Christian
traditions on the three issues which have been among the principal causes of division between the churches. It is therefore not
surprising that many Christians wonder why the church is still
so divided.

The recovery of the importance and deeper significance of the
eucharist has been one of the fruits of the liturgical movement
the origin of which is to be dated to the early part of this century
in the Roman Catholic church, and which has influenced the
whole church. In this way the revival of interest in liturgy has

1

encouraged the ecumenical movement. No longer is the eucharist considered simply as a liturgical rite, but as the expression of
the meaning both of the gospel and of the Christian life. So
Pannenberg can claim (1984:31)

> The rediscovery of the Eucharist may prove to be the
> most important event in Christian spirituality of our time,
> of more revolutionary importance than even the liturgi-
> cal renewal may realize.

The revival of interest in liturgy has not been confined to the
Protestant and Reformed traditions. Since the liturgical movement originated in the Roman Catholic church its fruits were
shown especially in the Constitution on the Sacred Liturgy of
the Second Vatican Council and in the reforms which have
resulted from it. One of the most important results is the understanding that liturgy is the action of the whole church:

> ... every liturgical celebration because it is an action of
> Christ the priest and of His Body the Church, is a sacred
> action surpassing all others (*Sacrosanctum Concilium*
> §7: Abbott & Gallagher 1966:141).

In the celebration of the eucharist the church re-discovers and
expresses its identity as the Body of Christ sent by the Lord to
promote healing and reconciliation. In societies such as South
Africa with deep social, economic, cultural and linguistic divisions the eucharist has a particularly important part to play in
recalling the church to its task of reconciliation.

The new shared understanding of the importance of the eucharist has meant that the eucharistic prayers of many Reformed and
Protestant churches are similar in theological expression to the
revised eucharistic prayers of the Roman Catholic church.
Some Anglican liturgies, for example (as in the case of the
Church of the Province of Southern Africa), have made use of
the Roman Catholic prayers with only minor amendments. An
illuminating collection of liturgical texts for baptism and eucharist has been compiled by Thurian and Wainwright (1983)
which shows the remarkable convergence between different
Christian traditions.

Much of this process has been due to a new understanding of

the meaning of sacrifice (Daly 1978; Ashby 1988), and particularly of the meaning of memorial (*anamnesis*), with its allusion to the Passover, the memorial or re-enactment of God's deliverance of Israel, his people. As a result there has been a tendency to go behind the controversies of the Reformation and get back to the eucharistic rites of the early centuries, especially to that ascribed to Hippolytus at the beginning of the third century. Although this is the first eucharistic rite of which we know, there are references to the eucharist and its importance in Justin (*Apol* 1:65-67) and in the Didache (9,10,14), which many scholars (J-P Audet 1958; H Chadwick 1967:47; JAT Robinson 1976:327) would date to the first century. There is a possible reference to it in Pliny (*ep* 10:96:7), who notes that one of the characteristics of Christians in Bithynia was "to meet together to take food, though it was common (*promiscuum*) food and harmless". By the second century at the latest therefore the eucharist seems to have been a regular feature of Christian life and worship.

The importance of baptism has never been doubted in the same way. However many different interpretations of its meaning have been advanced, it has generally been agreed that baptism is involved with membership of the Christian church. The argument of this book is an attempt to view baptism and the eucharist as characteristic marks of the Christian community from the beginning, by which Christians expressed their identity in distinction from Jews and others. With such an understanding we are to look at the fourth gospel through liturgical spectacles, and so try to discover a richer and fuller meaning in this enigmatic writing. We are concerned with the gospel as it stands, as the final editor apparently meant Christians to read and hear it, without 7:53 to 8:11 which is certainly a later insertion. In what follows "John" always refers to the final editor (or editors?) of the gospel, unless the context clearly indicates otherwise. This does not necessarily imply that the final editor was the apostle John.

The importance of signs

Human life is lived by signs, by the words which we utter and hear, or write and read, by the clothes we wear and the actions we perform. In the modern world the driver of a car is constantly directed by signs, either on the road or as given by other motorists. Every liturgical act of the church is itself a sign, or an aggregate of signs, being exemplified most richly in the Orthodox liturgy but found also in the simplest forms of Protestant worship.

Because of the rich diversity of signs and their uses, it is impossible adequately to classify them into different types. There is however an important distinction between two broad types of signs, which Perrin (1976:29-31) calls steno-symbols and tensive symbols. By steno-symbols he means signs which have a single, definite meaning, of which road-signs provide a good example: the red traffic light means "stop" and nothing else. The other type of signs, Perrin's tensive symbols, are those which need to be interpreted and given meaning by the observer, and though the sign itself has parameters beyond which one may not go, there are different ways of interpreting such signs. Every work of art – pictorial or literary – might be considered a tensive symbol, teasing the observer or reader to understand the meaning it conveys.

Even in the case of such tensive symbols, if a sign is to be intelligible it presupposes a common background shared by the one who uses the sign and those for whom it is meant. The clearest example is provided by language, which is a system of signs, vocal or written, which can be understood only by those who know the language. Similarly with patterns of behaviour or ritual acts: those who have been initiated into a particular social or religious group understand the meaning of the ritual and behaviour patterns which reflect the beliefs of the society. They live within a symbolic universe, whose signs can be understood by those who know the group's code and who share in its life. ·

Of all the different kinds of human societies and associations which have their own system of signs or symbols, religious groupings provide the clearest examples. Since their association is due entirely to their shared beliefs concerning the nature of

God and their own life, their beliefs are expressed in signs and rituals whose meaning they recognize and as a result of which their understanding of their beliefs is continually deepened. Whatever may have been the nature of the community for whom John wrote, the central issue for them, as for all Christians, especially in the early years of the life of the church, had to do with the person of Jesus Christ: How was he to be understood, and what was the meaning of his death on the cross? The writings of the New Testament are all concerned to explain the significance of the history of this man for Christian disciples and for the world. The four gospels provide a particular literary form of explanation: written in the form of a biography, they are different from the usual biography in their concern to express the meaning of Jesus for the communities for whom they wrote. In this sense they are like dramas whose purpose is to draw the reader or hearer to be closely involved in the story which they unfold, so that as form and redaction critical studies have shown, the story is as much a reflection of the circumstances in which the gospels were produced as a history of the events in Jesus' life. The gospels appear to have been written for those who were already Christians, who would have known the main facts about Jesus, but who may well not have been aware of their real significance.

In this respect the gospels show a resemblance to Greek tragedies, whose themes were the well-known ancient myths. The power of the drama was to be seen in the way it presented and interpreted these stories as drawing attention to the human predicament, so that the myths are shown to reflect the tragedy and drama of life at any time. Sophocles' *Antigone*, for example, raises religious, ethical and political issues which are as relevant today as when the play was first performed in the fifth century BC. Similarly, the evangelists tell the story of Jesus in terms which speak to Christians to help them see that the Jesus of whom the gospels speak is not a figure of past history, but the living Lord of the church. In this respect the gospels are like poetry or other literature in that the meaning is not simply fixed once for all but has continually to be discovered or rediscovered by the reader or hearer, who needs to share at least some of the attitudes of the evangelist.

The fourth gospel has all the marks of having been written later than the synoptics (*pace* Robinson 1985). Hengel (1989:3) would date it to the time of Trajan, about AD 100. Although it seems likely that John did not know the synoptic gospels, he was certainly acquainted with the traditions which lay behind them (cf Dodd 1963:423; Gardner-Smith 1938). The fourth gospel is a book of signs, not simply because it describes the signs which Jesus performed, but because it presents Jesus as the supreme sign, the revealer of God. The whole gospel revolves around this theme. As the Word of God Jesus is the sign of God's activity and revelation, and the declaration of his person. In the Old Testament, God's word was at work in creation (Is 55:10-11), in the Torah (Ps 119:105 – "Your word is a lamp for my feet", where the Hebrew *dabar* [word] is rendered by *nomos* [law] in LXX), and in the prophetic word where the prophet's words ("Thus says the Lord ...") are the signs of the words and the action of God. The Word of God made flesh (Jn 1:14) is the sign of the glory of God, and the only true revealer of God (1:18). The theme runs through the gospel: John 14:6-11 expresses it clearly – "He who has seen me has seen the Father" – and John 20:28, with the confession of Thomas, forms the climax of the gospel. Jesus is the sign of God, in the sense that he in his own person and activity is the manifestation of God. The signs which he performs point to and explain the meaning of his coming.

As the sign of God, Jesus is also the sign of life – of true life for the world, a theme developed especially in 1 John (1:1-2; 5:11-12), but clear enough in the gospel as well. Signs however as tensive symbols need to be interpreted: their meaning is not necessarily obvious to all, just as the significance of Jesus was not necessarily appreciated by those who saw him and heard him. The meaning of the sign depends on the attitude adopted by the observer: what the fourth gospel describes as "believing" (e g 1:12) expresses the attitude needed to understand the sign. Those who come with faith in Christ are able to see the meaning of the signs, and therefore to discover the meaning of life (2:11).

Similarly, those who have faith in Christ will understand the meaning of their acts of worship, which are themselves signs both of God's gracious action and of the worshippers' response of faith. In this sense the sacraments of the church can be considered to be occasions for realizing, and representing, the truth of the gospel, where as Barth put it (1969:72-75) the faithfulness of God is met by the faith of human beings. The argument of the following chapters is that John described the events of the gospel in terms which would have meaning for his readers or hearers who would recognize that what John described was being made present and significant for them in their own acts of worship. This was made possible through the power and presence of the Spirit with those who were met together in the name of Christ.

The method by which this is achieved is suggested by Culpepper, whose careful analysis of the literary design of the gospel shows how its meaning is to be found in the way by which the reader or hearer is drawn into the narrative. So the disciples are to be seen as "models or representatives with whom readers may identify" (1983:115). Such an understanding means that the readers of the gospel share a common world-view. They recognize, without having to be told, the allusions which John makes. Culpepper (1983:150) quotes PD Duke, who makes the point well:

> The wide use of irony in John's Gospel may indeed bear witness to a particular body of people who have lived long enough together with a shared faith, a shared practice, and a shared Beloved Disciple that a subtle manner of discourse is also shared. This gospel is their shared story. They know when to wink and when to weep. And they tell the story as they do that others might also know.

Martyn's description (1968:142) of the fourth gospel as a two-level drama is therefore very appropriate:

> The two-level drama makes clear that the Word's dwelling among us and our beholding his glory are not events which transpired only in the past .... These events to which John bears witness transpire on both the *einmalig* and the contemporary levels of the drama, or they do not transpire at all. In John's view, their transpiring on both levels of the drama is, to a large extent, the good news itself.

Kysar (1975:233) issues a warning: "Let the interpreter beware lest he ... find in the evangelist more theological sophistication than was ever intended". Nevertheless it seems clear that John was familiar with rabbinic exegetical methods, which certainly discovered in the text much more than appeared on the surface. John in fact used the Old Testament to explain the significance of the person of Christ and his death and resurrection (cf Manns 1985:538). A good example of his method is found in 8:56, "Abraham your father was overjoyed to see my day, and he saw and was glad", leading up to the claim of Jesus in 8:58 "Before Abraham existed, I am". Barrett (1978:352) draws attention to a rabbinic understanding that Abraham was shown the days of the Messiah. This was a deduction from Genesis 24:1 (*ba' bayyamîm*) which means that Abraham was "well advanced in years" (RSV), but which literally means "he entered the days", and this was taken to refer to the days of the Messiah. So John follows this up, and claims that what Abraham saw was the day of Jesus the Messiah. Such an interpretation makes good sense of an otherwise obscure passage. If John expected his readers or hearers to understand this allusion, those for whom he wrote must have been looking out for signs of deeper meanings. Nor should this be thought surprising in an age when people *listened* to the story of Jesus rather than read it for themselves. As they heard it read they savoured the words and language used, and were affected by their power. The stories achieved the same effect as that described by Steinbeck (1966:285) in his novel of the cotton-fields of America in the Great Depression – "The story tellers, gathering attention into their tales, spoke in great rhythms, spoke in great words because the tales were great, and the listeners became great through them".

Alter (1989:13) draws attention to the allusive character of the Hebrew bible, which he compares with "the pervasive allusiveness of Eliot's *The Waste Land* or Joyce's *Ulysses*" rather than with "the occasional allusiveness of Wordsworth's *The Prelude*". The writers of the Hebrew bible could rely on their hearers' acquaintance with the formative events of Israel's history, and with the traditional narratives about them. So Alter goes on to stress the importance of familiarity with the original texts: "... a close study of these writings in the original discovers again and again, on every level from word choice and sentence structure to the deployment of large units of composition, a delight in the manifold exercise of literary craftsmanship" (1987:15).

The Old Testament was the bible of the church in the early years, and the gospels all assume knowledge among their audience of the Old Testament background. As the story of Jesus was read aloud the hearers were led to see allusions to various themes of the Old Testament. But they also were helped to see allusions to their own life as disciples of Christ. The text resonated with their own experience. In discovering this for themselves they found that the words and the stories had more meaning than was at first apparent. They themselves became part of the story of Jesus. Christians who shared in a common life would note the congruence between the gospel narrative and their liturgical acts which brought the meaning of the gospel alive to them.

John in his narrative uses various techniques to display the relevance of the gospel for believers of his own day, and in so doing he enables believers of later ages too to find meaning in the gospel. He achieves his purpose by his constant allusions to the Old Testament, which he sees as being fulfilled in Christ (e g 5:39). But it is the contention of the following chapters that he is also continually helping his audience to recognize more clearly the meaning of the liturgical acts by which they show themselves to be God's own people (1:11). Certainly the gospel can be profitably read against the background of the church's worship even if John did not consciously intend this (cf Wakefield: 1985).

This book is an attempt to show that it is likely that the allusions to baptism and eucharist were there from the start, and that they would have been appreciated by the community for which John wrote, just as they can be appreciated by today's reader or hearer.

1

The liturgical character of the fourth gospel

Religious texts contain a mystery; the mystery is somehow encoded in the text; it is decodable.

If we want to know what the Evangelists were getting at in their assertion that there are mysteries in the text – hidden meanings which are other than the superficial apparent meanings – then we need to pay close attention to this context of normal use (*sc* in Christian Church ceremonial).

E Leach in Leach E & Aycock DA *Structural interpretations of biblical myth* (CUP 1983) 2 & 97

Introduction

The liturgical character of the fourth gospel has long been recognized, though the exact nature of its concern with the liturgy has been differently assessed. Guilding (1960) in a verit-able *tour de force* argues that the structure of the gospel is based very firmly on the Jewish lectionary system for feasts, but Morris (1964) rightly draws attention to the many hypotheses which her argument entails. Though it may be the right answer, it is certainly not the only possible one, and in view of many loose ends it seems to be an unlikely solution.

Cullmann (1953) saw John to be so interested in the sacraments that he interpreted many of the pericopai with direct reference to baptism and eucharist. Although this would appear to be a move in the right direction, Cullmann brings to the fore what is better seen as reflecting the background out of which John wrote (cf Borgen 1965:190). Cullmann is right to note the importance of liturgy in the New Testament church (1953:33-34). Anthropologists generally tend to believe that the ritual precedes the myth: that is to say, the fixed pattern of ritual and worship comes first, as an interpretation of the facts which are recalled and set forth, and then there follow the narratives which interpret both the fact on which they are based and the liturgical action (cf Leach 1983a:17). This view would be supported by the understanding of Trocmé (1983) of the origins of the Passion Narrative. He argues that the archetypal Passion Narrative arose from the celebration of the death of Jesus by Christian Jews at the time of Passover, when they are likely to have done what Jesus did on the night before he died "in his memory" (*eis ten emen anamnesin*, 1 Cor 11:24,25). The Passion Narrative for Christians therefore took the place of the Passover Narrative (*Haggadah*) for Jews, just as the eucharist was always interpreted in terms of the Passover, even though the Last Supper may not have been a Passover meal. Certainly this would help to explain both the similarities and the differences between the Passion Narratives as presented by Mark (followed by Matthew), Luke and John. If we note too the importance of the liturgical practices for the people of the Old Testament, shown especially in the celebration of the Passover and the Day of Atonement, it is clear that scripture and the liturgy hung so closely together that Eliade (1979:335) can say of Israel "In the last analysis, *the liturgical practice renews the structures of the world*" (italics original). If then the death and the resurrection of Christ are taken to be the events by which God established a new relationship and a new covenant with his people, the solemn *anamnesis* of this in the eucharist is the continual renewal of the relationship, and takes the place both of the Passover and of the Day of Atonement.

The New Testament frequently emphasizes the importance of the liturgical observances, shown not only in such passages as

Acts 2:42, which we may see as Luke's idealized picture of the early Christian community at Jerusalem, and therefore elsewhere too, but also in passages like 1 Corinthians 11:23-32 and Romans 6:1-11, where it is to be noted that on neither occasion does Paul attempt to explain either the eucharist or baptism. He simply takes it for granted that his readers will be familiar with these rites, so that he can appeal to them for support for his argument in each case. Further, 1 Corinthians 11:23 clearly shows Paul's conviction that his understanding of the eucharist was derived from the Lord. We may note the technical terms used (*paralambanein*, receive; *paradidonai*, hand over), which describe the solemn transmission of teaching. Presumably Paul meant not that he had received a direct revelation from the risen Christ, but that he had no doubt that the practices which he found in the church really did come direct from the Lord. There would therefore be no grounds for thinking that the celebration of the eucharist at Corinth was markedly different from its celebration in other centres, even though, as Audet (1958:406) believes, Gentile churches may have laid more stress on its nature as a communal feast (*agape*) whereas Jewish Christians may have stressed its redemptive nature along the lines of the Passover. It is worth while recalling that had it not been for the squabbles at Corinth we would not have had Paul's description of what he thought ought to be the meaning of the eucharist and his understanding of its institution.

Even more significant is Paul's appeal to the eucharist in 1 Corinthians 10:14-21 to support his argument. He has been warning the Christians at Corinth to beware of giving the impression that they were guilty of idolatry by eating meat which had been sacrificed to idols (8:4-13) for fear of causing other disciples to sin. Then after the digression in chapter 9 in which he defends his own behaviour he reverts in chapter 10 to the theme of idolatry. In view of verses 14 to 21, the opening verses (vv2-4) clearly allude to baptism and eucharist. But the important passage follows the reference to the Old Testament types. "Avoid idolatry. I am speaking to sensible people: determine for yourselves what I am saying" (vv14-15). He then goes straight on to refer to the eucharist as providing a clear example of his argument. Although the words refer to the unity of Christians with one another (v17), their main thrust is to show the way in which the eucharist expresses the unity of the believer with Christ (vv16,20-21). Paul therefore can assume that the wayward Corinthians will at least know the meaning of the eucharist which they celebrate. Similarly Luke 24:35 is to be seen not as a historical record of the actual words of the two disciples but rather as a reminder to the reader that the risen Lord is always to be found in the "breaking of the bread". Other passages in the gospels (e g Mk 6:35-44 par; Mk 14:22-25 par) are similarly to be understood in the light of the liturgical practices of the church at the time when the gospels were written.

In view of all this, therefore, it is likely that John especially, being the latest of the gospels, and perhaps written about AD 100, took for granted certain liturgical practices among those to whom he wrote. In any attempt to reconsider the influence of the liturgy on John, and so to find some help in the interpretation of the gospel, there are four preliminary points which must be borne in mind.

1   Sacraments in the New Testament

The use of the word "sacrament" is tendentious and anachronistic. At any rate since the Reformation, sacramentalism has often been taken to connote a form of expression of the gospel which is opposed to the preaching of the word, as though it described some kind of automatic, if not magical, way by which the grace of God could be transmitted to the worshipper. On a view like this the sacraments are often – and rightly – regarded as a distortion of the gospel. Such a view overlooks the importance of the faith of the recipient which, from the human side, completes the relationship effected by the Lord through his grace (Schillebeeckx 1963:19f). There is no evidence that John thought of baptism and eucharist as *in themselves* conferring on their recipients the grace of God. Käsemann therefore may be right (1968:77) in claiming that John was protesting against some kind of institutional sacramentalism which had arisen in the community for which he was writing. The difficulty, however, in determining the situation and circumstances of the author of the fourth gospel renders such a conclusion uncertain. It may be that Käsemann has himself fallen into the error of which he warned others of indulging in eisegesis. Certainly his principle that "It is not proper to read our expectations into the text of John, so long as a non-sacramental interpretation is possible" (1968:32) displays an *a priori* assumption that non-sacramental interpretations are intrinsically superior. Käsemann's comment seems to be based on his understanding of sacraments in a post-Reformation church. Much more reasonable is the view expressed by Moule (1956:4) that "The sacraments were the vehicles of the Gospel, and the Gospel was sacramental, and the two are virtually inseparable". This general comment on the New Testament is specially relevant to our theme. Now Käsemann is perfectly justified in asking exegetes not to read their own expectations into the text – whether these are sacramental or otherwise. An essential element in any approach to the text is an awareness by the interpreter of his or her own presuppositions or pre-understanding. Bultmann (1955a:253-256) rightly sees the hermeneutical process as involving a continual process of correcting one's pre-understanding. It is neither right nor possible to come to the text without any presuppositions. The kind of openness of mind that is needed is the ability to recognize our presuppositions and to discern the way in which our opinions need to be revised as a result of a careful listening to the text and its message. The work of interpretation can be successful only in so far as the interpreter is prepared to enter into dialogue with the text and to carry on the dialogue which has been constantly going on between the church and the bible through the centuries.

When dealing with John therefore we need to note the danger of talking of "sacraments", for the word does not occur in the New Testament, even though the Latin word *sacramentum* is sometimes used in the Vulgate as a translation of the Greek *musterion* (Eph 1:9; 3:3,9; 5:32; Col 1:27; 1 Tim 3:16; Rev 1:20; 17:7), though not with its later meaning. (It is a matter of interest that the *Nova Vulgata Bibliorum Sanctorum Editio* of 1979 retains *sacramentum* only in Eph 5:32 and 1 Tim 3:16, changing to *mysterium* in the other passages.) *Sacramentum* was originally used in two senses: as a juridical term it referred to the sum

deposited by each of two litigants which was forfeited by the
loser of the law-suit. (Isidore in the seventh century called it
sponsionis pignus, the pledge of a mutual agreement, *Orig* 5:24.)
As a military term it referred to the oath taken by the soldier on
enlistment in the army. Its first use in a Christian context is in
the pagan author Pliny (*ep* 10:96:7) of about AD 115. Pliny may
indeed have picked up a Christian technical term already in use,
but he presumably understood it as referring to a Christian's
oath of loyalty to Christ. In this sense it would seem to represent
the Latin equivalent of the Greek *eperotema* (1 Pet 3:21) and
refer to the pledge of loyalty made by the candidate at baptism
as the NEB takes it, though Tripp (1981) believes otherwise.
Sacramentum seems to have a similar meaning in Tertullian, and
the word came into regular use to refer to the sacraments of the
church in the third century. The Greek term to describe the
liturgical practices of the church is *ta musteria* (the mysteries).
This term expresses more clearly the relationship between the
"mystery of Christ" (Eph 3:4; Rom 16:25, *to musterion Christou*)
– by which is meant the incarnation, death, resurrection and
ascension of Jesus – and the representation (= making present
again) of this act of salvation in baptism and eucharist. To speak
in this way certainly avoids the charge of institutionalism, for
"the mystery of Christ" is really a way of describing not something hidden, but rather the purpose of God for his world now
disclosed once for all in Jesus Christ. It would be tempting to
ask whether this is the reference in Mark 4:11 (cf Leach
1983b:100-111).

It is therefore wise to refrain from talking about John and the
sacraments since such language tends to beg the question. It is
preferable to think of John and the worship of the church, with
special reference to baptism and eucharist. In this connection
it is worth while recalling the perceptive comments of Barrett
(1950:15). He points out that John surrendered historicity and
yet remained faithful to the gospel

  because he firmly fixed the new dominical teaching of the
  Holy Spirit to the focal points of Christian worship: to
  baptism, in which the life of the kingdom is conveyed; to
  the eucharist, in which it is continually renewed; and to
  the preached word, by which the truth judges and re-

deems the world; while in them all the historic acts of
Jesus are called to mind and proclaimed.

Once, however, we have noted the danger of the word "sacrament" in this connection, there seems good reason to recognize
the liturgical background of the fourth gospel.

2   For whom did John write?

The second preliminary point concerns the problem of discovering John's intended audience. For whom did he write, and
from where? Of the various answers given to these questions
those of Brown (1966:lxxi) seem most likely. The gospel (as was
presumably the case with the other three gospels) was written
primarily for Christians. In drawing attention to the use of the
term "the Jews" in John, Brown concludes that it is "almost the
technical title for the religious authorities, particularly those in
Jerusalem, who were hostile to Jesus". Although it must be
noted that on occasion the term is used simply in a descriptive
sense without any such connotation, Brown argues that John's
regular use seems to reflect not the period of Jesus' ministry but
the time when the gospel was written when there was conflict
between Jews and Christians. The evangelist wrote not so much
to convert the Jews – for perhaps it was already too late for this
to be a viable option on a large scale – as to show Christians the
strength of their claim to be the true successors of the people of
the Torah, and to confirm them in their faith (20:31). Quite
clearly John expected his audience to be familiar with the Old
Testament: without this background much of the gospel would
have been unintelligible. In fact very often the allusions are such
that they could scarcely be appreciated by anyone who did not
have a deep knowledge and understanding of at least parts of
the Old Testament scriptures. If therefore he was not writing
primarily to commend the faith to Jews – and his way of talking
of the Jews seems to be such as to preclude this (e g 8:41-47) –
it would seem that he was writing for a Christian community
which used the Old Testament as a basis for its faith in Jesus.
John was then concerned to draw out the meaning of the Old
Testament for this community and to show how its hope was

fulfilled in the coming of Christ.

In drawing out the meaning of the Old Testament as finding its fulfilment in Christ, John would also need to explain the significance of Jewish worship which was likewise transformed by the coming of Christ. Guilding's view (1960:55) that the new order of worship of Jesus and *his* church (*ekklesia* Mt 16:18) rendered the Old Testament *ekklesia* (Dt 23:2 LXX) void is too extreme. There was a very real continuity between the worship of the synagogue and that of the Christian church, which is well described by Bouyer (1966:21-34). Although the earliest text which we have of synagogue worship, *Amran Gaon*, is of the ninth century, Bouyer argues that it broadly represents the form of synagogue worship current in New Testament times. He bases his argument not only on the innate conservatism of Jewish worship, but also on the way in which the prayers reflect not the Jewish theology of the high Middle Ages but that of Judaism contemporary with Christian origins, and in this respect he notes the similarity with the prayers of the Qumran community. The early date of these Jewish prayers is supported by allusions and references in earlier writers, and by the recurrence of similar themes in early Christian liturgies. Bouyer shows the close parallels which exist between the eucharistic prayer of the early liturgies and the prayer of the synagogue. There is of course a fundamental difference between them, insofar as the eucharistic prayer is centred on Christ, whose coming and work are seen as the fulfilment and transformation of Judaism.

The early Christians therefore had liturgical models ready to hand, and if they were already differentiated from Jews at the time when the gospel was written, their common liturgical celebrations served to mark them off from non-believing Jews. These liturgical celebrations would be largely modelled on Jewish forms, but they would differ from them in their attention to Jesus and his work, since it is his claims which caused the break with Judaism. If John then was writing for Christians it can be presumed that they would be familiar with the liturgical rites which formed part of the expression of their faith in Christ. He would not have to spell these out, and his allusions to them would be easily picked up, because of the common background from which both the author and his audience came. So, for example, it would seem reasonable to hold that John 6:34 – "Lord, always give us this bread" (*kurie, pantote dos hemin ton arton touton*) – would call to mind the petition from the Lord's Prayer (Lk 11:3; Mt 6:11). There the unusual word *epiousion* (normally rendered "daily") indicates, because of its rarity, that this was already part of the liturgical language of the church. Chapter 17, as will be seen later, also contains allusions to the Lord's Prayer. The prayer seems to have been a mark of the disciples of Jesus, thereby performing a function similar to that which John the Baptist taught his disciples (Lk 11:1-2; cf Mt 6:9; Did 8:2).

The "symbolic world" in which John wrote was determined especially, though obviously not exclusively, by these two factors, the world of the Old Testament, with the Torah, the narratives, the traditions and all that went to make up Judaism, and the early Christians' experience of Jesus. Both factors came to expression in story, or myth, and in liturgical rites. The stories were continually rehearsed by the community by reciting them and by sharing in the rituals which expressed their meaning. Johnson (1986:14) clearly describes the relationship between story and ritual:

> In society's myths, we find the linguistic expression of its deepest self-understanding: how it has come to be, why it is different from others, what its future is. The recital of these myths renews the rituals of the society, and the rituals make evident the "truth" of the myths. The myths and the rituals make each other work, and because they do, they enable the life of the group to continue.

Examples of this principle can be found in societies diverse in character and in time. McAllister (1981) for example, describes the rituals of incorporation in the Gcaleka tribe in the Transkei, celebrated with beer-drinking and the slaughter of an animal. There the rituals and the oratory form what is termed "a restricted code" signalling "the normative arrangements of a group" based upon "common knowledge, accepted values and behaviour patterns, ... shared ideals and basic cultural forms" (1981:45). Kilpatrick (1983:74-75) refers to a description by M Fortes of "an observance current among an African people, the Tallensi", in which in symbolic fashion "the first arrival of the founding ancestor of the chiefly clans and his reception by the aboriginal Earth-priests" is recapitulated. By the celebration of the ritual and the recitation of the "charter-story" or myth, the people assert their identity and recognize their origin.

Similarly, in a different context Cohen (1985) describes the symbolic rites by which the people of Whalsay in the Shetland Isles express the consciousness of their cultural identity. The symbols which they use are boundary-markers, the significance of which is apparent only to the participants. "They are symbolic statements designed to perpetuate the boundary, not to demolish it" (Cohen 1985:309). Such symbolic statements become all the more important when a community is under threat, in this case the threat of absorption into the wider technological society of modern culture.

The same situation existed in the time of the New Testament, of which a clear example is provided by the Qumran community. Here detailed rules governed the admission of members into the community. After being finally admitted the members took part in the community meals, celebrated in a symbolic and liturgical manner (*1QS* 6 = Vermes 1987:69-70):

> Whenever there are ten men of the Council of the Community there shall not lack a Priest among them. And they shall sit before him according to their rank and shall be asked their counsel in all things in that order. And when the table has been prepared for eating, and the new wine for drinking, the priest shall be the first to stretch out his hand to bless the first-fruits of the bread and the new wine.

A more extended ritual is described in the *Messianic Rule* (*1QSa* = Vermes 1987:102), suggesting that from the first the new community of Christians is likely to have had its own distinctive liturgical rites.

All these examples are interestingly concerned with eating and/or drinking – the Gcaleka with beer-drinking, the Tallensi with beer and flour, the people of Whalsay especially with whisky-sipping from a single glass and with food, and the Qumran community with bread and wine. Kilpatrick (1983:59-61) also draws attention to the Jewish romance, *Joseph and Asenath*, where the God-fearing man, the Jew, is described as he who "eats the blessed bread of life and drinks the blessed cup of immortality". He therefore cannot eat the bread and drink the cup of idols (cf 1 Cor 10:21).

In all these examples participation in the meal indicated membership of a common society. Not only was the meaning of the meal appreciated solely by members of the group, but the meal itself helped to bind the group together and to assure the members of their common identity and purpose. It is therefore no wonder that a meal should be a central symbol for the early Christians who had to differentiate themselves from other Jews and (as a result of the admission of Gentiles) to show that they had both a valid origin and a valid claim to be a community distinct from the Jews, however much they were indebted to them. Not surprisingly therefore the Didache (9:5) prescribed:

> Let no-one eat or drink of your eucharist except those who have been baptized in the name of the Lord.

This rule, which has been followed by most of the church throughout the centuries, is not meant to be exclusive so much as to mark off those who belong from those who have not yet been admitted to the new community.

Bishop Stephen Neill (1968:195-196), writing from his experience in India, described a situation somewhat analogous to that of the New Testament:

> A high-caste Hindu may go almost any length in the direction of Christian faith and obedience, provided that he stops short of baptism. He may read the Bible and pray. He may even attend Christian worship, and still ... he will be permitted to remain in his family. If, however, he is baptized, the whole situation is changed. Inward conviction is a man's own private concern, but to belong to two religious *communities* is impossible. The convert becomes to his own family as one dead; in many cases the funeral rites will be performed for him, so that dying and rising again acquires for him a most poignant significance.

In the rites of baptism and eucharist the early Christian church recognized both its parentage in Judaism and the new factor in Jesus which differentiated it from Judaism. By their faith in Christ crucified, risen and ascended members were bonded together with a common faith and a common hope.

John is therefore concerned to point out that just as the Old Testament can now be properly understood only with reference to Jesus (see especially Jn 5:39-47), so also the meaning of all the liturgical rites which the church celebrates is to be found in him and his work. If this is so then we have a principle to guide us in the interpretation of the gospel which can be of real value today. For although we must not read into John the practices of the twentieth (or even of the fourth) century, the basic elements of baptism and eucharist, as well as their essential meaning, are sufficiently clear to enable us to read John and understand him from a background which *in some ways* is similar to those for whom he wrote, in so far as the Christian church is founded upon the act of God in Christ, and in word and ritual continually sets forth its basic creed.

3   Baptism and eucharist in the New Testament

What then do we find in the New Testament about baptism and the eucharist? We are here concerned not with a detailed analysis of all that is involved, or indeed of the different understandings which were very likely current at the end of the first century in different parts of the church, but rather with the basic elements of the rites as they appear in the New Testament. If we can find an underlying pattern of baptism and eucharist in other books of the New Testament, we can use this as an experimental basis for interpreting John. If a consistent pattern then emerges, it would seem reasonable to hold that John was written from such a background. Similarly such a study may help us reach not only a better understanding of John, but also of the meaning of baptism and eucharist in the church today.

The word *baptizein* and cognates is sometimes used with its original meaning "to wash" or "to dip" (Mk 7:4; Lk 11:38; cf 2 Kg 5:14 LXX). Its use in a Christian sense draws attention not to the rite itself but to the object of the action of washing or dipping. So Christian baptism is described as baptism *into* Christ (Gal 3:27; Rom 6:3 as rendered in NRSV) or into the name of Christ, where the phrase "in the name of" (*eis to onoma*) probably means "into the possession of" (Ac 8:16; 19:5). The use of the phrase with the name of the Trinity in Matthew 28:19 has the same meaning. The one who has been made a disciple by baptism now belongs to God – Father, Son and Holy Spirit. This sense of a change of ownership is shown by the use of the language of slave (*doulos*) and master (*kurios*) and the corresponding verbs, especially as used in Romans 6:6-23. In this way there is a clear contrast made by Paul between Christian baptism and baptism into Moses (1 Cor 10:2), just as Acts 19:3,5 distinguishes between John's baptism and Christian baptism by reference to the object of the rite.

The Pauline texts (Rom 6:1-11; Col 2:12-15; 2:20-3:4) make it clear that the meaning of baptism is inseparably associated with the death and resurrection of Jesus Christ, and that it is the occasion when what is really a single composite event is reproduced in the life of believers, as they now embark on their new life "in Christ". This new beginning signified by baptism can be regarded in two ways. On the one hand it is due entirely to the call and the grace of God: this is to be noted in the frequent use of *kalein* (to call) in the aorist tense to denote the beginning of the believer's life in Christ (e g Rom 8:30; 9:24; 1 Cor 1:9 *et saep* – cf the same use in 1 Pet 1:15; 2:9,21; etc), as well as in the use of the perfect or aorist of such verbs as *dikaioun* (to justify, Rom 8:30; 1 Cor 6:11; Tit 3:7), *hagiazein* (to sanctify or to make one a member of God's own people, 1 Cor 1:2; 6:11) and possibly *chriein* (to anoint, to christen, or, as later writers put it, to make one *alter Christus*, a second Christ, 2 Cor 1:21; cf 1 Jn 2:20,27). Even the passive forms in Romans 6:3-4 and Colossians 2:12 indicate that it is God who effects the change.

But on the other hand baptism demands the response of faith by the believer. From this point of view the beginning of the Christian life can be dated from the time when faith in Christ is expressed, shown in the New Testament by the frequent use of the aorist of *pisteuein* (to believe), which thus comes to mean "to make one's act of faith". This describes the human part of the act of baptism whereby a person starts on the new life of faith (e g Rom 10:14; 13:11; 1 Cor 3:5; 15:2,11).

In neither case is there an understanding of baptism as a *mere* ritual act which in itself effects salvation. Certainly, since it expressed the action of God, there is a supernatural element involved in it, but baptism is above all else the rite which establishes a new relationship which is dependent for its fulfilment both on the initiative of God and on the human response. Further, baptism marks the *beginning* of this new relationship, which constantly needs to be re-affirmed by reference to God's saving act in Christ and the expression of faith in God by the believer. It is therefore no wonder that the eucharist came to be seen as the regular way in which this relationship between God and believers is continually expressed and deepened. There is no indication in the New Testament that baptism itself could ever be repeated. The statements in *Baptism, eucharist and ministry* of the World Council of Churches (1982:4-5) represent the New Testament position:

> Baptism is an unrepeatable act. Any practice which might be interpreted as "re-baptism" must be avoided. (§13)
> Baptism needs to be constantly reaffirmed. The most obvious form of such reaffirmation is the celebration of the eucharist. (*Commentary* §14 (c))

The consequence of this is that in the New Testament the proper meaning of baptism is to be seen in the case of adults. This, however, does not necessarily imply that infant baptism was not practised in the New Testament period or that the development of infant baptism in the early church was a misunderstanding of the nature of baptism and of the evidence of scripture.

In the New Testament Christian baptism is always associated with the gift of the Holy Spirit (Mk 1:8 par; Ac 2:38; 19:2f), and therefore is seen to have eschatological implications (2 Cor 1:21f; Eph 1:13f). It is the beginning of a new life in Christ which is to lead on to the final consummation of life with Christ in God.

One further point is everywhere assumed: Christian baptism always means entry into a community, the church, described by Paul as the Body of Christ. Baptism into Christ, therefore, is a corporate rite, by which the candidate is involved in a new life in fellowship with others who are similarly united with Christ. The act of becoming a Christian in the New Testament involves repentance (*metanoia*), meaning a new life and change of direction; faith, the positive aspect of repentance by which obedience is promised to Christ; and baptism in water into the name of Christ or of the Trinity. Although neither *metanoia* (repentance) nor the corresponding verb is found in the fourth gospel, the underlying idea is certainly present.

The eucharist, like baptism, is not often mentioned in the New Testament. There was no need to do so, since it was a regular part of the Christian life. It was very closely connected in meaning with the Passover as a feast of deliverance and an occasion for blessing God. But the feature which differentiated Christians from Jews was their belief in the death and resurrection of Jesus Christ. Just as the meaning of baptism was derived from the cross and resurrection, so the meaning of the eucharist, though modelled on the Passover, was found in the making present of the act of God's love in Christ which was the basis of the believers' life in Christ and in the Christian community. This is indicated in the accounts of the institution of the eucharist in the synoptic gospels and in 1 Corinthians.

The use of the word *anamnesis* (1 Cor 11:24-25) is especially instructive. Thurian (1960-61) and von Allmen (1969:c 1) among others have stressed the significance of the concept of *anamnesis* as meaning much more than a memorial of a past event. The word recalls similar language regarding the Passover whereby the participants did not simply commemorate what happened to their ancestors but also saw themselves as involved in God's act of redemption. In the same way the Christian eucharist becomes the way in which the redemption effected by Christ in his death and resurrection is proclaimed and made present for the participants. This recovery of the biblical understanding of *anamnesis* has resulted in the remarkable ecumenical convergence in eucharistic theology noted above (pp 1f). Like baptism, the eucharist recalls the death and resurrection of Christ and is the expression of the community's common faith in Christ as they are united in the act of sharing in the one loaf and the one cup (1 Cor 10:16-17). Every eucharist therefore, from the human side, is the occasion for the renewal of faith in Christ and the pledge of the believer's loyalty to him, and is an expression of the corporate nature of the community in Christ. It is not surprising that many early, and later, liturgies include a reference to Romans 12:1, which is full of cultic phrases – "... present yourselves as a sacrifice (*thusia*), living, holy (*hagia*), and well-pleasing (*euarestos*) to God. This is the worship (*latreia*) demanded of you (*logike*)".

The eucharist does not recall the Last Supper but the cross and resurrection of Christ (1 Cor 11:26; cf 5:7), and is the summary of the meaning of the incarnation from the conception to the ascension. The Last Supper points forward to, and finds its meaning in, the cross and resurrection. Every eucharist derives its meaning from the same event. The accounts of the institution of the eucharist furnish to the church the authority to recall the death and resurrection of Christ by using bread and wine. Just as Christian baptism derives its significance from the object of the rite (the person of Christ, or the Trinity), so there is no meaning in the bread and wine apart from their reference to the death and resurrection of Jesus Christ.

All accounts of the institution of the eucharist (Mk 14:22-24; Mt 26:26-28; Lk 22:17-19; 1 Cor 11:23-25) indicate it as a way in which the Lord assures his presence to his disciples. The very act of eating together was a potent sign of unity and shared life, both among Jews (Gal 2:11-14) and pagans. MacMullen (1981:39) states that "the idea that a god might join worshippers who were eating together was widely diffused, most overtly in celebrations called *lectisternia*, when the icon was brought out of its house and was laid on a couch beside the celebrants". The celebration of the Christian eucharist was the sign not only of the risen Lord's presence with his people, but also of their sharing in his person and life (1 Cor 10:16-21). It is unlikely that any of the writers believed in an actual change in the elements, or that they would adopt the later description used by Ignatius, "the medicine of immortality" (*Eph* 20:2, *pharmakon athanasias*). Nevertheless, all understand that the Lord is present with his people in the eucharist. Luke's description of the meeting of the two disciples with the risen Lord on the Emmaus road vividly portrays the recognition of the Lord's presence in the breaking of the bread (24:31,35). The earliest Christians believed that in the eucharist there was a true meeting with Jesus, a *koinonia* with him (1 Cor 10:16), in which their own identity as his body was re-affirmed.

This is confirmed by two other features in the account of the Last Supper and related incidents – the covenant and the peace. The covenant (*diatheke*) is mentioned by Mark (14:24), by Matthew (26:28), by Luke (both in the longer text, 22:20, and in verbal form in 22:29) and by Paul (1 Cor 11:25). The reference here is both to the establishment of the covenant made through Moses (Ex 24:8) and (especially in Paul and Luke) to the new covenant promised by Jeremiah 31:31-34. It is worth noting that the phrase "the new covenant" (*he kaine diatheke*) is used by the writers of the New Testament only with reference either to Jeremiah 31 or to the eucharist. Jeremiah 31:33 links it with the creation of the new people of God:

> This is the covenant which I will make with the house of Israel after those days, says the LORD: I will put my law (*torah*) within them, and I will write it upon their hearts; and I will be their God and they shall be my people (RSV).

The person of Jesus, through the Spirit, takes the place of the *torah*, and the eucharist is the occasion when his presence with his people is affirmed.

The idea of peace (*šalôm*) is linked with the covenant in the Old Testament, and in four places there occurs the phrase "my covenant of peace" or "the covenant of my peace" (Num 25:12; Is 54:10; Ezk 34:25; 37:26). The message of the gospel is especially the proclamation of this peace of God to the Gentiles, which was seen to be the fulfilment of such prophecies as Zechariah 9:10 "He will speak peace to the Gentiles (nations, *goyim*)". In all the early liturgies which we possess the Peace of Christ was symbolically given by the president to the participants, and was usually called "the kiss of peace" or the *agape* (Justin *Apol* 1:65; Athenagoras *Suppl* 32). In the New Testament there are similar references which often occur together with other liturgical phrases, though not necessarily in the context of the eucharist (Rom 16:16; 1 Cor 16:20; 2 Cor 13:12; 1 Th 5:26;

1 Pet 5:14), and John 14:27 refers to the new quality of the peace which Jesus gives. The giving of the Peace at the eucharist therefore reinforces the understanding of the presence of the Lord with his people as they celebrate their redemption gained through the Lord's death and resurrection.

The Peace has the further meaning, both for Paul and for later writers and liturgies, of affirming the unity in the peace of Christ of all who share in it. It thus helps to emphasize the meaning of the eucharist (as indeed of baptism) as the expression and confirmation of the unity (*koinonia*) of all who accept the lordship of Christ. 1 Corinthians 10:17 displays the ease with which Paul moves from the idea of participation in Christ (v16) to that of the unity of all who are so sharing in Christ. This theme is emphasized by the twofold meaning of "body of Christ" (*soma Christou*). It is no accident that the phrase used with reference to the eucharist (1 Cor 10:16; 11:24,27,29) occurs again with clear reference to the church in 1 Corinthians 12:12,27. It was for this very reason that Paul condemned the Christians at Corinth. "Not discerning the body" (1 Cor 11:29) would seem to refer especially to Christians as being the body of Christ. The behaviour of the Corinthians when celebrating the Lord's Supper was a denial both of their calling and of the meaning of the Supper.

The same theme of fellowship and unity is present in Luke 22:21-34, where it is dramatically set forth in a number of contrasting scenes (cf Marshall 1978:818). We may note especially the part played by Judas (Lk 22:21-23), who becomes the type of all who share in the eucharist and yet deny by their subsequent actions their unity with the Lord and with one another. This is vividly described by all the evangelists, and by Paul's use of the imperfect (*paredideto*) in 1 Corinthians 11:23 as contrasted with the following aorists. This strictly should be translated "was being handed over". The Lord gave himself to death (Gal 2:20; Eph 5:2, where in both instances the same verb is used as that which describes the action of Judas) at the same time as Judas, the disciple whom he chose, was handing him over to his enemies. It is noteworthy that this imperfect tense is retained, without exception, in all the Greek liturgies. All these various facets of the eucharist need to be remembered as we consider the fourth gospel.

4 Scripture and community

There is a further preliminary point to bear in mind. John presumably did not think of himself as writing scripture: he saw in Jesus the fulfilment of the Law and the Prophets. What they pointed to had now arrived in the person of Jesus (Jn 5:45-47). The scriptures of the Old Testament were authoritative for the Jew, but their purpose for the Christian was now different: they served simply to point people to Jesus Christ. Like the Torah in the restricted sense of the Pentateuch, the Old Testament as a whole could be seen as the *paidagogos* (the slave who took the boy to school) to bring people to Christ (Gal 3:24). This is not to deny the continuing importance of the Old Testament, but because Jesus Christ is now the centre and goal of faith, faith in him becomes the key for the interpretation of scripture, and the words and acts of Jesus transcend in importance those of Moses. Jesus does not take the place of God to whom the Old Testament bears witness: he reveals and declares him through his life and through his cross, and through his Spirit in the continuing life of the church (cf Küng 1978:132; Denis 1973:50).

For this reason *traditio* (Latin for the Greek *paradosis*), the solemn *handing on* of the church's teaching from person to person, church to church, generation to generation, may never be neglected. For Christ's will is made known in the community, the church, and has continually to be checked and confirmed or changed by reference to the words and actions of Jesus as the New Testament records them, and to the Old Testament as providing the witness to the meaning of Jesus Christ in the whole story of God's dealings with his people. For John, as for Paul, the preaching of the word is the preaching of Christ: to him the scriptures bear witness and church's worship proclaims him. There is no contrast in the New Testament between word and sacrament: to preach the word means to preach the gospel, and every celebration of the eucharist is likewise a preaching of the word, since it is the proclamation of the loving act of God in Christ. In fact, if the task of hermeneutics is to make present the meaning of actions described in the scriptures, the celebration of the eucharist is itself the clearest example of the hermeneutical endeavour, where the act of God in Christ located at a moment in time is constantly set forth and made a present reality for those who share in it.

In a later century Calvin referred to the sacrament as *verbum visibile* (a visible word). This does not mean that the sacrament is merely the sign of a past event, any more than the scriptures are merely a historical record. Sacraments and preaching, when duly administered, as the Reformers insisted, effect a change in the recipient or hearer and lead to a deepening of that faith and commitment which the gospel demands. John's purpose is to try to resolve the complexity of the relationship between the acts of Christ, the faith of human beings and the worship and preaching of the church. He himself acts as an interpreter of the words and acts of Christ, so that the evangelist is himself engaged in hermeneutics. He writes his gospel therefore to show that the Word who became flesh is incarnate now in the community, the church, through his Spirit who leads his church into all the truth (16:13). The church's worship in baptism and eucharist is part of the continual process by which the gospel is both heard and proclaimed so that it may be more deeply understood with all its implications, in the life of the Christian community today.

Lohse (1961:122-123) recognizes that there could not have been a Christian congregation which did not baptize or meet for the Lord's Supper. But he argues that the fourth evangelist deliberately omitted all references to the sacraments in order to show that the acceptance or rejection of Jesus occurs in the acceptance or rejection of his word, which challenges the hearer or reader. Those references in the gospel which Lohse accepts as referring to baptism or eucharist (3:5; 6:51-58; 19:34) are regarded as ecclesiastical redactions. Lohse admits (1961:124) that there is no direct argument *against* the sacraments in the fourth gospel, but that John's stress on the cross and exaltation of Jesus is so pronounced as to preclude mention of baptism and eucharist.

The following chapters interpret the evidence of the fourth gospel in rather a different way, arguing that John was not primarily concerned either to defend the importance of the worship of the church or to play it down. Rather, he accepted it as part and parcel of the church's life, and he wrote his gospel to show that the church's liturgical practices, like the witness of the Old Testament, have no meaning apart from God's action in Jesus. They were rather ways in which the action of God in Christ was made effective and significant for Christian disciples as they expressed or renewed their faith in the Word of God incarnate in Christ. Lohse believes that the fourth gospel was written for this purpose. Such a purpose however is in fact reinforced, and not contradicted, by the understanding of baptism and eucharist which John seems to have.

Brown (1965:62) issues a wise warning:

> If there is no clear indication in the Gospel itself that a passage has a symbolic reference to a sacrament, and if there is no evidence in the early Church that the passage was understood sacramentally, then we may well rule out a sacramental exegesis. A sacramental symbol that the Evangelist intended to be easily understood without explanation should have left some trace in art or in liturgy or in the writings of the Fathers. Without such assurance, we may suspect that we are dealing with modern imaginative eisegesis.

Nevertheless, John's general allusive style of writing means that it is only rarely that symbols and statements are clearly explained. John 2:21 and 7:39 are exceptions rather than the rule, and in each of these two examples further interpretation is necessary. Brown believes that there must at least be "some internal, contextual indication" of sacramental symbolism (1965:66) before such an exegesis can be accepted. The problem here is to determine the nature and extent of the "contextual indication" which is considered necessary. Is there, for example, a clear enough indication in John 8:56 that the author intended an allusion to Genesis 24:1, as has already been suggested (p 8)? The criteria should serve as warnings not so much to avoid as to discipline the use of imagination in the exegesis of the fourth gospel.

Niewalda (1958:22) expresses his belief that the principal sacramental allusions in John have not been, and cannot be, proved by exegesis. Nevertheless, because sacramental allusions were frequently recognized by early writers, he believes that sacramental symbolism was there from the first and that it provides the best key to understand the fourth gospel (1958:164-169). Since the allusions would be picked up by the readers or hearers of the gospel, explicit explanation would have been superfluous (1958:19). Although we need to recognize the danger of claiming to discover a single key to unlock the secrets of the fourth gospel, it is reasonable to hold that its *Sitz im Leben* is to be found in the worshipping life of the early church, and especially, as Grundmann believes (1959:69), in the Lord's Supper as the continuing expression of the community's being.

The fourth gospel "is a book for insiders ... One of the primary functions of the book, therefore, must have been to provide a reinforcement for the community's social identity" (Meeks 1986:163). Such reinforcement is especially provided by corporate liturgical actions. It is with this supposition that the following chapters examine some texts from the fourth gospel, as a result of which it is suggested that real coherence is shown by John as he relates the experience of his church to the historical life of Jesus. Some of the texts as we now have them, notably John 3:1-12 and 6:26-58, can scarcely be interpreted without seeing an allusion to baptism or eucharist. But even in these instances there is no explicit mention of either, perhaps because John deliberately wished to focus attention on the need of faith in Jesus the Messiah rather than on the ways in which faith was liturgically expressed. Once allusions to baptism and eucharist are admitted in some places in the gospel, it becomes reasonable to examine the possibility that such allusions are to be found elsewhere too. The evidence is cumulative and circumstantial. As the conclusion cannot be exegetically proved, the reader alone must determine how satisfying it may be and how far such an interpretation may enrich our understanding of baptism and eucharist "as meaningful pointers to the meaning of the life of Christ and Christian discipleship" (Paschal 1981:176).

2

The sign of greater things to come: John 2:1-11

... the evangelist says a great deal without actually
saying it ... What seems clear and simple on the
surface is never so simple for the perceptive reader
because of the opacity and complexity of the
gospel's sub-surface signals.

R A Culpepper *Anatomy of the Fourth Gospel*
(Fortress 1983) 151

Signs in the fourth gospel

The signs in the fourth gospel have always been seen to possess
special importance. Though it has often been postulated that
John used some kind of "Book of signs" source for his gospel,
this is not necessarily the case. The whole of the fourth gospel
is an urgent plea to the reader to see in the life of Christ the
action of God himself, so that Jesus is presented especially as
the revealer of God (1:18; 14:9f; 20:28). In this sense Jesus is
himself the sign of God's action in the world, the visible evidence
of the nature and activity of God. The call to faith is sounded
throughout the gospel (1:12; 20:31), and the disciple is challenged to find in Jesus the fulfilment of the Old Testament and
of God's plans for his world. It is not that the actual person of
Jesus provided incontrovertible evidence of the presence and

33

action of God. "Come and see" (e g 1:46) is the first stage which needs to be complemented by the profession of faith "you are the Son of God; you are the king of Israel" (1:49). To have meaning the sign has to be accepted as pointing to, if not manifesting, the reality which it signifies.

But if Jesus is himself the sign of God's action, his acts are also signs, and the evangelist is at pains to show the importance and significance of the signs as means of describing not only who Jesus was in his incarnate life, but who he is now in the ongoing life of the church. Hanson (1975:30) therefore regards the signs in John as performing a similar function to the sacraments in the life of the church – "opportunities for faith in which the nature and action of God may be grasped by faith". In themselves they are ambiguous, but when properly appreciated they are ways of revealing the glory of God displayed in Jesus Christ. This does not mean that the signs in the fourth gospel are always or necessarily connected with the acts of Christian worship, but since they perform a function similar to that of the church's liturgy it would not be surprising to find that they contain allusions to those acts with which Christians would be familiar.

Dodd (1954:6) accepts the view "that the gospel has behind it the common Christianity of the early period, and that readers who shared the life and thought of the church would find here much that was familiar, from which they could advance to its new and unfamiliar teaching". The first sign which John describes is one which (like the miraculous feeding of c 6) was full of meaning for Jews. Goodenough (1965:129) claims "that from the rabbis themselves we know that the blessing and eating of bread and the blessing and drinking of wine had by Philo's time become highly important Jewish observances", and he goes on to note that "Philo says that only one purified may be told about the sacred mystic rites, since what in them is manifest to the sight would mean nothing unless one could see beyond the perceptible to the immaterial and conceptual existence behind what is seen". This would seem to be very much in keeping with John's approach: the *meaning* of the ritual acts could easily be misunderstood. It is not surprising that the *disciplina arcani* of the early centuries meant that only the baptized were permitted to know of what went on in Christian liturgical assemblies, a practice enjoined even by the Didache (9:5). John, with his understanding that signs were of value only to those who had eyes to see, is therefore likely to have referred to the liturgical rites in ways by which their meaning is ever being made more vivid to the participants, while those who have not come to faith must remain in ignorance.

If this is the way John went to work it is not surprising that commentators have felt either that John has no interest in the sacraments or that his gospel is entirely sacramental. Smalley, for example (1978:204-210), tends to play down the importance of the sacraments in John. MacGregor on the other hand can write (1963:119) "John is rightly regarded as the supreme teacher on the sacraments". Similarly Corell (1958:47) believes that the gospel "reflects the seething life of the early Christian Church, a life which found its main expression in liturgy and teaching". The liturgical actions describe the way in which God's revelation has been understood and accepted. As John therefore presents the gospel of Christ it is natural that he should take for granted the liturgical rites of the early church, and seek to draw out their meaning for the benefit of his hearers and readers.

He effected this not by writing a biography of Jesus, but by selecting those incidents which in truth or in tradition were associated with him and which depicted in dramatic form the meaning of his words and deeds for those for whom John wrote. This dramatic quality of the gospel may never be neglected. In this way, as with all good drama, the reader becomes a participant and not only an observer. The fourth gospel presents a drama of the revelation of God. Though it has a beginning and an end the intervening scenes are composed in such a way that they portray a developing picture of the revelation of God in Christ. Each of them contains within itself the message of the whole (Dodd 1954:383), but each successive pericope adds a further feature to the total picture, so that the wealth of the gospel is all the more clearly disclosed by the subtle differences of emphasis employed. So in our examination of 2:1-11 we see it in relation to the whole, as arising from the context of the Old Testament now reinterpreted in the light of Christ and as speaking to Christians of John's day – and therefore to Christians of every day.

There is no need here to attempt to distinguish the sources which John used, nor to distinguish his own changes and additions. Fortna (1970) has attempted this in great detail. We are concerned rather with the meaning which John assigns to the story as it now appears, and though our knowledge of this would be greatly enhanced if we could be certain of the form in which John received the story, even the careful analysis of Fortna must be seen as yielding only tentative results. In fact, Fortna believes (1970:102-109) that John has so drastically re-ordered the signs that it is his contribution which is the really significant factor. A reasonable historical background for the story of 2:1-11 is suggested by Derrett (1963) who describes the obligations incurred by guests at Jewish weddings and argues that Jesus at the right time unexpectedly contributed the abundance of wine on behalf of himself and his disciples which custom would have demanded of him. Though this may indeed furnish the historical setting, anxiety to recover this may well lead to a failure to comprehend the real meaning of the narrative as it stands.

The context of the first sign

This first sign (*semeion*) in the gospel might be described as marking the end of the introduction. Just as the Prologue proper (1:1-18) introduces the whole gospel, as it indicates themes which are to be developed throughout the gospel, so this sign foreshadows the future glory to be revealed in Jesus. Jesus is not only the content of the gospel (as Mk 1:1 would have it), but the author of all creation (Jn 1:1). This claim is to be substantiated by his works (5:36), which are seen as signs of his true work on the cross and in the resurrection. Boismard (1956:14f) believes that the period from the baptism of Jesus (1:19) up to 2:11 is a carefully structured programme of seven days, and that the sign of Cana takes place on the seventh day. In view of the importance which Philo assigns to the seventh day (as will be indicated later), if Boismard's programme is correct, then the climax of the week is reached in 2:1-11.

The first sign therefore is of great importance: it is itself *arche* (the beginning – 2:11). As the word is here used predicatively it does not need the article. Though most manuscripts insert it, the best witnesses favour its omission. Fortna (1970:35f) believes that the reading of P⁶⁶* *tauten proten archen* (this first beginning) is original, and that the "all but intolerable Greek" which this reading gives is due to John's addition of *archen* to his source. More likely *proten* (first) was a gloss, later incorporated into the text either before *archen* or (with S*) after *Galilaias*. In any case this sign is not just the first of a series: it is the archetype of all signs, which declare the glory of the Word incarnate and are intended to lead people to faith in him (cf Barrett 1978:193). If it should be thought that this contradicts what has been said above, in so far as John seems to have been writing for Christians, it should be remembered that faith is not simply a once for all event: the expression of faith is an ongoing process. Past, present and future are inextricably linked in the life of every human being. "Just as a man still is what he always was, so he already is what he will become" (Jung 1978:323). John is concerned to help Christians become what by God's grace they already are. The faith which they expressed in their baptism needs continually to be fostered and enriched. The aorists *ephanerosen* (he manifested) and *episteusan* (they believed) in 2:11 indicate the actual results of the sign. So the greatest sign of all, the cross and resurrection, is followed by the statement of the purpose of the gospel in 20:31 – "that you may believe that Jesus is the Christ, the Son of God, and that by believing you may have life in his name".

The pericope has been preceded by the story of the coming of Nathanael to Jesus, to which it is linked especially by the use of the phrase "the third day" (*te hemera te trite* 2:1), the significance of which will be further discussed below. This phrase follows three references to "the next day" (*te epaurion* – 1:29,35,43) and indicates the end of a series of incidents. Another indication of the link between 2:1-11 and the story of Nathanael is given in 21:2 by the reference to "Nathanael of Cana in Galilee". Nathanael and Cana belong together. The account of Nathanael shows, *inter alia*, that the true Jew, the true Israelite in whom there is no guile (unlike Jacob, the original Israel) is the one who comes to Jesus. Boismard (1956:21) draws attention to the repetition in the opening chapters of John of the words *come*, *find* and especially *see*. Seeing and believing is a theme which runs right through the gospel and is exploited by John in various ways. The theme adds a further element to the importance of Nathanael. He comes to Jesus by God's grace (Heb *Nathanael* = gift of God): for Jesus knew him even before he was summoned by Philip, while, like an assiduous rabbi, he was under the fig tree, the right place to study Torah. Here at the start of the gospel we are given an example of God's gracious call to people in Christ (cf 15:16). In coming to Jesus Nathanael fulfils the destiny of Israel. The name Israel, as Boismard (1956:99f) convincingly demonstrates, was regularly (though wrongly) thought to mean "man seeing God". Philip's invitation to Nathanael "Come and see" (1:46) is the occasion for the fulfilment of Israel's destiny.

But the fourth gospel can never be analysed in such a way as to pin upon any text a single interpretation. In the story of Nathanael we have a pattern which reappears in 2:1-11, with an apparent change of referent in the narrative. On the one hand Nathanael is the true Israelite, but his address to Jesus shows his recognition of Jesus as the true rabbi and the true king of Israel, which prepares the way for the disclosure of Jesus as the true Israel. The vision of God granted to Jacob (Gen 28:12) finds its fulfilment in Jesus (1:51), for, as 1:18 puts it, the only one who has truly seen God is the Son, who alone can reveal the vision to others: Jesus is truly "man seeing God". The Hebrew text of Genesis 28:12 could mean that the angels were ascending and descending either on the ladder or on Jacob, though the Septuagint takes it to refer to the ladder. The rabbis recognized this double meaning, and one interpretation connected it with Isaiah 49:3 "You are my servant, Israel, in whom I will be glorified" (NRSV), a theme repeated in verse 5. Odeberg (1974:33-40) quotes *Genesis Rabbah* 68:18, where Jacob's dream is interpreted as showing the link between the ideal Israel in heaven and Israel on earth. The glory of the heavenly Israel, and therefore the glory of God, is reflected in earthly Israel. The glory is now revealed in Jesus (cf 1:14), so that in place of Jacob John writes "the Son of Man" the usual self-designation of Jesus. As the rabbis connected Genesis 28:12 with the glorification of Israel, God's servant, so now Jesus takes the place of Israel. He becomes the true image, the real human person. It is in the history of this man, this connecting link between heaven and earth, that the glory of God is to be manifested, and it is this glory that the fourth gospel expounds.

The nature of the glory is hinted at in 1:50 – "you will see greater things than these", where the singular person (*opse*) is to be noted, followed almost immediately by the plural *opsesthe*. The greater things are to be seen not only by Nathanael, but by all who recognize Jesus as the king of Israel whose glory will be shown in the cross and resurrection, anticipated now in the sign which follows. The readers and hearers are in this way invited to become those who truly see God and so show themselves to be the true Israel (cf Boismard 1956:164f).

The first sign from a liturgical perspective

The account begins with the words "on the third day" (*te hemera te trite* – 2:1). It would be pedantic (in spite of Schnackenburg 1968:325) to think that this refers to a definite temporal period and nothing more. Following Old Testament usage (cf Daly 1978:184) the phrase indicates an event of importance. It is used in the Old Testament to refer to the binding of Isaac, marking the decisive time for the offering (Gen 22:4), where the Septuagint has it in the same form as here – *te hemera te trite*. In Hosea 6:2 the phrase is used of the day of resurrection for Israel, to which perhaps Luke 24:46 refers. John could scarcely be unaware of its regular use to refer to the resurrection of Jesus (Mt 16:21; 17:23; 20:19; 27:64; Lk 9:22; 18:33; 24:7,46; Ac 10:40; 1 Cor 15:4). 1 Corinthians 15:4 is specially instructive (cf Boismard 1956:106f), since this is part of a credal statement incorporating the phrase in the same form as in John 2:1 (where it should however be noted that a few manuscripts have the more usual *te trite hemera*).

The phrase immediately draws attention to Sunday as the day not only on which Jesus rose from the dead, but also on which the church celebrates the resurrection in its worship (Ac 20:7), as would seem to be shown particularly in John 20:19. The story of Nathanael has prepared the way for the manifestation of the glory of Christ, and the opening words of chapter 2 are rich in symbolic meanings. So the next word *gamos* (wedding) evokes festal and eucharistic images. It is frequently used in the Septuagint to translate the Hebrew *mišteh* (feast), which is used in Isaiah 25:6 to refer to the Messianic banquet of the Lord. (The LXX is here more of a paraphrase and *mišteh* is not represented.) In the New Testament *gamos* is regularly used with an eschatological reference (Mt 22:2-12; 25:10; Lk 12:36). The Lukan parallel to Matthew 22 (Lk 14:16) speaks of a great supper (*deipnon mega*): apparently the banquet is more important than the marriage. Both ideas are brought together in Revelation 19:7-9 where the marriage-supper of the Lamb is the symbolic representation of the messianic banquet, centring upon the crucified and risen Lamb of God, and where the use of *deipnon* can scarcely fail to recall the Lord's Supper with its eschatological reference (1 Cor 11:20,26). The first few words of the chapter are therefore already rich in eucharistic allusions. The importance of the whole account is shown by the backward reference to it at 4:46, at the beginning of the account of the second sign. Only the first two signs are numbered (2:11; 4:54), and the connection of the second sign to the first enables the reader to see the importance of the complete series of signs which Cana initiates and which leads up to the cross and resurrection.

We are next told that the mother of Jesus was there. She is mentioned before Jesus himself, and in the fourth gospel she appears only in this chapter (vv1,3,5,12) and in 19:25-27. In both places she is addressed as *gunai* (woman), an unusual address by a son to his mother. Brown (1966:107-109; cf Brown *et al* 1978:188) suggests that the allusion may be to Mary as the new Eve, a view earlier proposed by Vawter (1956:160) who sees an inevitable allusion to Genesis 3:20 LXX – "Adam called the name of the woman *Zoe* (life), because she is the mother of all the living". Certainly John 19:25-27 shows, as Origen recognized (*Comm in ev Ioh* I:4; Preuschen 1903:8f), that the disciple now occupies the place of Jesus: those who share in the life which he gives can call Mary their mother too. Guilding (1960:183) interestingly notes that John 2:1-11 reflects the vocabulary of the

Genesis lections for the month Kisleu (*gemizein*, fill, 45:17 only; *methuein*, drink, Gen 43:34; *archioinochoos*, chief wine-steward, and similar compounds in Gen 41:9f; and the command of v5 in Gen 41:55, a command given in response to a shortage of food). More significant however is the appearance of Jesus' mother only here and at the cross. In this way John establishes the connection between this sign and the crucifixion as the true place of the revelation of the glory of Christ. Such a view is greatly strengthened by verse 4 – "my hour has not yet come".

Jesus too had been invited to the marriage, and his disciples. The grammatical structure is interesting: the subject of *eklethe* (was invited) is Jesus, and the disciples are added almost as an afterthought, as though Jesus is the one who matters but who cannot be understood without them – a view reflected throughout the gospel, shown especially in 15:1-10 and 17:20-26. Even though this was a not uncommon Septuagintalism (e g 2 Kg 18:26 LXX), and is found elsewhere in the fourth gospel, it still serves to present Jesus as the real subject of the verb. In the same way in the eucharist the Lord is present always with his disciples, without whom there can be no supper.

When the wine had run out his mother appealed to Jesus. Certain inconsistencies in the narrative suggest, according to Lindars (1970), that there is here a combination of a miraculous story of changing water into wine and a parable (vv9f) indicating the superiority of the new wine over the old (cf Mk 2:22). Lindars suggests that the miracle story may have originated from among those told of Jesus in his earlier years, though Derrett (1963:94f) prefers the view already mentioned. In many ways the story plays a similar part to that of Luke 2:41-51, where the independence of Jesus from his parents is asserted (Lk 2:49), even though he remains subject to them.

Wine is frequently mentioned in the Old Testament, especially in connection with festive and significant occasions. It played an important part in the weekly *kiddûsh* ceremony, as well as in the annual Passover. The rabbis thought of it especially as the symbol of the Torah (Dodd 1954:84). By its very nature, writes Boismard (1956:139), wine can symbolize the joy of the messianic renewal. The eschatological reference of Isaiah 25:6 mentions wine, where the Septuagint reads "they will drink gladness, they will drink wine" with reference to the messianic banquet. Goodenough (1965:127) notes that rabbinic exegesis often assigned messianic connotations to wine. Whether or not John was influenced by the Greek rites of Dionysus (Bultmann 1963:238), or by Philo's allegorical treatment (Hoskyns 1947:192) he could not have failed to be aware of the rich imagery associated with wine in the Old Testament.

The wine had run out (v3). A few manuscripts have the longer reading "they did not have any wine because the wine of the wedding had been used up". Though Bultmann (1971:116) believes this to be original, it is more likely that it is a somewhat clumsy attempt to spell out the meaning of the genitive absolute (*husteresantos oinou*). The lack of wine is the occasion for the exchange between Jesus and his mother. Jesus' words "what have you to do with me" (as RSV renders *ti emoi kai soi*) have provoked much discussion (see, e g Derrett 1963:89-92; Boismard 1956:144-147). It is a literal translation of a Hebrew phrase which can scarcely be rendered literally into English – "what to me and to you". Derrett believes that the phrase can mean "Between us there can be no quarrel", and that it denotes "a protestation of a deep unity of ideas and motives", and he adduces in support a corresponding phrase from modern Kurdistan with exactly the same form and meaning. It is however clear that often the phrase denotes some difference between the speakers and is an implied rebuke. Does John make deliberate use of this ambivalent phrase? On the one hand Jesus is asserting that his ministry is to be carried on independently of Mary his mother, and on the other he is telling his mother that her concern will be attended to by himself. Here is a new era in the history of salvation. The wine of the Jews, the Torah, the Covenant, had run its course and was to be superseded by the wine which Jesus would provide.

The reply of Jesus is not simply the assertion of his independence: "my hour has not yet come" looks forward to the hour of glory on the cross (12:27-33; 13:1; 17:1). Cullmann (1953:67) compares the similar theme in 7:2-6, where Jesus' moment, his *kairos*, still in the future, is contrasted with that of his brothers. It is on the cross that the glory of the Lord will be seen in its true and proper light, and the archetypal sign of Cana introduces the first reference to a motif which is carried on throughout the gospel. The allusions of 2:1 are thus more sharply depicted by the reference to the hour of Jesus. But even now the Lord is at work, and his mother's injunction to the servants indicates her support for the work which her son now begins independently of her. The words used are exactly the same as those spoken by Pharaoh to the Egyptians during their time of famine. Pharaoh told them to go to Joseph. Here at Cana at the start of the gospel the reputed son of another Joseph (1:45) supplies the needs of those who are celebrating a marriage, the sign of the way in which Israel's true bridegroom is to bring joy to his people.

The word *diakonos* (vv5,9), corresponding to the Latin *minister*, has both a general sense of "servant", and also a cultic meaning among Christians (1 Tim 3:8-13) and pagans alike (Moulton & Milligan 1914-1929:149), and its use here is presumably coloured by its liturgical associations. Perhaps even the *architriklinos* (vv8f) as the chief butler in charge of the servants (Schnackenburg 1968:333) or the master of ceremonies (Derrett 1963:88) connotes the president of the eucharist. Certainly the next sentence quite explicitly refers to cultic features. The six jars are described as "placed there in accordance with the purification rites of the Jews".

Philo (*LegAll* I.1-18) has much to say about the number six, which he calls the perfect number (3). The mortal things (*ta thneta*) which God creates correspond to the number six, but the things of blessedness and happiness (*ta makaria kai eudaimona*) correspond to the number seven (4). The importance of this for human life and behaviour is described as follows (16); "When the holy *logos* in accordance with the number seven comes upon the soul, then the number six, together with all the mortal things the soul seems to make with it, comes to a halt". Something of this understanding may be present here, especially in view of a similar theme in 5:17-18, where the continuing creative work of God is declared to be carried on by Jesus ("my Father is working until now, and I (*ego*) am working"). If this allusion can be seen in 2:6, then the six jars symbolize not the total ineffectiveness of the Jewish ritual and cult, but rather its failure to attain to the full perfection which is to be found only with Jesus the Messiah, the true *logos*.

According to John, purification (*katharismos*, v6) results from the action of Jesus (13:10) or his word (15:3) or his blood, that is, his death on the cross (1 Jn 1:7). The references in the gospel are all found in liturgical contexts. In 2:6 the reference is to Jewish rites of purification, good enough in their limited way, but now to be transcended by the action of Christ, as surely as the water with which the jars are to be filled will be found to be inferior to the wine which will be drawn from them. It is possible that *katharismos* alludes to Jewish proselyte baptism, as Jewish sources suggest according to Beckwith (1978:44), whereby the proselyte is purified and so able to participate in the Passover (*Pesahim* 8:8; Danby 1933:148). The importance of the distinction between clean and unclean is everywhere shown in the Mishna. This is reflected too in the scriptures, so that Ezekiel (36:25) looks forward to the time of real purification – "I shall sprinkle pure (*katharos*) water upon you and you will be cleansed (*katharisthesesthe*) from all your impurities (*akatharsion*)". This seems to have been regarded as a type of baptism by Hebrews 10:22, if not by John 3:5, and it may be that the reference in John 2:6 is to Christian baptism as drawing its meaning from the death of Christ (cf Cullmann 1953:70). Since both baptism and eucharist express the significance of the cross and resurrection, it would be unwise to limit the allusion here to the eucharist. John 13:1-20 similarly alludes both to baptism and eucharist, and is intimately connected with the Passion Narrative.

The size of the jars (containing between 80 and 120 litres each) and their being filled to the brim indicate the abundance of the wine provided at the marriage-feast, comparable to the abundance of food provided by the Lord at the feeding of the five thousand (6:13). The benefits of the Lord's passion are incalculable. It is only when the wine has been drawn from the jars and tasted that the *architriklinos* makes his comment, which is the punch-line of the narrative – "you (*su*) have kept the good wine until now". This sentence, like 2:4b, contains the clue to the meaning of the narrative. However valuable has been all that God has done in the past in and to his people, the real provision of his grace is now to be found in Jesus and his action.

The *architriklinos* calls the bridegroom (*numphios*) who has not been mentioned previously. In Mark 2:19f "the bridegroom" clearly contains a reference to the Messiah, and it is to be noted that this saying occurs near to that about the new wine (Mk 2:22). Narratives in the gospels, and especially in John, cannot always be precisely and definitively analysed and pinned down. Images which are apparently mutually inconsistent tend to be used. So on this occasion, at the start of the narrative Jesus is clearly not the bridegroom: but he is the provider of the new wine, and in 2:10 the bridegroom is seen as the provider of the new wine. The tantalising shift of referent gives a vitality to the account which renders it capable of different interpretations. This apparent inconsistency may be seen as one of the marks that John has brought together different traditions, but it is the finished product with which we are concerned.

The use of *numphios* with a messianic connotation is found not only elsewhere in the New Testament (Mk 2:19f par; Mt 25:1-13; cf Rev 21:2,9; 22:17) but also in John 3:29 so that it would seem to be an inevitable conclusion that the reference here is to Jesus both as the provider of the new and better wine (wine which is not only better but is described in absolute terms as "the good wine"), and also as the promised Messiah. The wine is regularly connected with the death of Christ and the eucharist. Although the eucharistic cup is not referred to in the New Testament as "the wine", but always as "the cup" (*to poterion*), the correspondence of the wine with the blood of Christ is demanded by such passages as John 6:53-56, and the connection of wine with the Passion of Christ is shown by 15:1-13 (especially v13) and 18:11. Since the messiahship of Jesus is declared especially in the cross and resurrection the connection of the bridegroom with the wine is doubly significant. So the contrast in 2:10 between "everyone else" and "you" is very marked: the actions of the true bridegroom are unlike those of anyone else, for the true bridegroom has declared his love to the uttermost on the cross. In this way the reader is shown the glory of God, anticipated in this sign but to be shown in Jesus throughout the gospel and to reach its culmination in the cross and resurrection.

So this sign, unlike most, is not followed by a discourse. Its meaning is rather indicated and reinforced by a succession of events. These events might themselves deserve the name of signs. Certainly 3:2 refers to "signs" even though John specifically numbers the second sign only at 4:54. The first sign occurs in Galilee, but the scene soon changes to Jerusalem (2:13, where the reference to the proximity of the Passover helps to display the liturgical context). The first sign indicated the renewal which Jesus came to bring to the Jewish cult and worship. The account of the cleansing of the Temple is a messianic act of purification (cf Mal 3:1-3). His action is questioned with the words "what sign do you show us for doing these things?" (2:18). The reader knows that the sign has already been given at Cana. Jesus' reply to the question plays the same part in this narrative as the words of the *architriklinos* in 2:10. "Destroy this temple (*naos*) and in three days I shall raise it up" (2:19) is, as is made explicit in verse 21, a reference to his own person. The centre of the Jewish system of worship, faith and life is to be transferred from the Temple to the person of Jesus, who is shown by the resurrection to be what he claims to be (v22).

The first sign as an introduction to the gospel

The theme of the fulfilment of the Old Testament promises is carried on throughout the gospel. But it is not simply fulfilment: however perfect the Old Testament dispensation was – and John would not wish to deny its value – it is now superseded by the advent of the *logos* incarnate who brings an altogether new dimension into the relationship between God and his people. The scriptures all pointed to Jesus and his work (5:39): this theme is presented in one form or another in most of the pericopai of the fourth gospel. It is clearly shown in 2:1-11, set as it is between the story of Nathanael and that of the cleansing of the Temple.

All three pericopai allude to the cross. Jesus will be shown to be truly king (1:49) only on the cross (19:19-22). What Nathanael saw was only the beginning. The miracle of Cana is the sign of greater things to come, which will be manifested only at the arrival of Jesus' hour. Similarly the meaning of the cleansing of the Temple will be clear only in the light of the resurrection. The same theme runs throughout the gospel: Jesus is greater than Jacob (4:12), greater than Abraham (8:53), the true vine (15:1) and the bearer of the grace and truth which the Torah was meant to convey but which is to be found only in Jesus. It is as though the thrust of the fourth gospel is to convince its readers that those who have put their faith in Jesus the Messiah are the true people of God (cf Brown 1966:lxxviii), and that those who have refused to acknowledge Jesus have forfeited the right to be considered Abraham's descendants (3:36). John 8:37-47 expresses the position clearly: if the Jews were truly Abraham's descendants they would accept the word of Jesus (*ton logon ton emon* – v43), for the word (that is, the Torah) which they had been given by God through Moses finds its real expression in Jesus, the Word incarnate. To seek to kill Jesus (v40) therefore clearly shows the disbelieving Jews to be no longer the descendants of Abraham. The argument is similar to that of Paul in Galatians 3:6-29 or Romans 4.

Though the fulfilment of the Old Testament in Jesus is one consistent theme in John, there is another of equal importance running through the whole gospel. This is the situation of the community for whom John wrote. At a time when there was no New Testament canon, the followers of Jesus expressed their faith in him by their common life, both by meeting the ethical demands of the gospel which they had accepted, marked particularly by their display of unity and mutual love (13:34f; 17:20-23), and in the liturgical practices which helped to bind the members of the community together as the expression of the basis of their faith, and as the means of renewing their commitment to the Lord.

John therefore wrote with this twofold thrust – fulfilment of the Old Testament *and* the present experience of Christ through the Spirit in the common life of the community. The fourth gospel is not meant therefore to be a historical record, at least in the modern sense of the term. Whatever John may have thought happened at Cana, he told the story in a way which best describes the meaning of the gospel proclaimed by Jesus. He bridged the gap between the Old Testament promises and the time of the church by constant allusions to its liturgy, so that the words and stories shed light on the meaning of the community's liturgical actions.

John 2:1-11 is all about the new life. As an introduction to the signs of Jesus it not only looks forward to their consummation on the cross, but by its allusions to baptism and eucharist it reminds believers that the worship in which they engage is itself a sure sign not only of what God has done in Christ but also of what he will do in their lives and in the life of the world. The eucharistic allusions are clear for all those who have eyes to see – the third day, the marriage-feast, the deacons, the wine, the bridegroom as the supplier of the new wine. So too is the connection with the Passion. The hour of Jesus can be only foreshadowed at Cana. But the hour of the marriage-feast, like the hour of a woman in labour, will bring to the disciples the true joy which cannot be taken away from them (16:21f). So the sign of which 2:11 speaks is the sign of the death and resurrection of Jesus, the greater things which Nathanael has been promised. But with its eucharistic, if not its baptismal, allusions it displays the Christian liturgy as the link in the present between the past historical act of God in Christ and the future hope, already assured yet still to be realized. The promise made to Nathanael – "you will see greater things than these" (1:50) – is thus renewed to every participant in the eucharist as he or she acknowledges the Lordship of Christ, shares in his mission and even begins to experience his joy.

Such a view helps us to see the liturgy of the church in the right perspective. It is never an end in itself, for the meaning of all Christian worship is derived from the person of Jesus Christ who by his life, death and resurrection declares the glory of God. To share in the glory of God in the liturgy is therefore to recognize the obligation and privilege to share in Christ's service to the world. The meaning of this first sign is continually developed throughout the gospel, with subtle allusions to the church's worship to help disciples see its meaning and implications.

3

The new creation: John 3

The simplicity and truthfulness of the symbols was
at times terribly apparent, to the extent that each
man interpreted them according to his own needs
and level.

P White *Voss* (Eyre & Spottiswoode 1957) 298
(with reference to aboriginal cave paintings)

Jesus and Nicodemus

Chapter 2 of the gospel has plenty of references to liturgy. Apart
from 2:1-11 there is the reference to the Passover in verses 13
and 23, and the incident of the cleansing of the Temple in verses
14 to 22. These two themes are connected. As Jesus is to be seen
as the new Temple, the new centre and focus of worship, so the
gospel will also show him to be the true Passover Lamb (19:36).
The meaning of Jesus and his work is further expressed in
chapters 3 and 4.

Chapter 2 of the gospel ends with a double use of the word
anthropos, man in the sense of a human being. Jesus is himself
contrasted with men and is represented as having knowledge of
"what is in man, human beings". In the next verse (3:1) "a man
from the Pharisees", Nicodemus by name, comes to Jesus. In
this way he is presented as a representative human being, and
also as a representative Pharisee finding his goal in Jesus. His

approach to Jesus "by night" signifies his tentative understanding of the meaning of the signs and of the person of Jesus,
whom he recognizes as a teacher come from God. Though he
comes by night, he comes paradoxically to the light, though his
recognition of this occurs only later. The story of Nicodemus is
the story of every person, and especially of the Jew, who eventually finds his destiny in taking the body, the person, of Christ
(19:39, see Suggit 1981). As a ruler of the Jews and as a Pharisee
he becomes the symbol of the hopes and aspirations of Judaism.
Jesus' reply to Nicodemus' address seems on the face of it to
have little connection with what Nicodemus said. Yet it is intimately related. For John means the reader to understand that
the meaning both of the signs and of Jesus can be appreciated
only by those who have been given a new view of life. The
importance of Jesus' words is marked by the double *amen* (v3),
and by their elaboration in verse 5.

The requirement is to be born from above (*anothen*). *Anothen*
can mean both "again" and "from above", but John's primary
meaning is certainly "from above", as is made clear in 3:31,
where the one who comes *anothen* is contrasted with the one
who comes "from the earth". Only by being born *anothen* can
one "see the kingdom of God" and so experience God's kingly
rule (Bultmann 1971:134). Verse 3 (repeated in different words
in v5) contains the only reference in the fourth gospel to the
kingdom or reign of God. The theme of Jesus' reign or kingship
has already been mentioned in 1:49, when Nathanael who came
to Jesus addressed him as king of Israel. The only other references in the gospel to Jesus as king (apart from a passing
reference in 6:15) are found in the account of the triumphal
entry into Jerusalem (12:13,15) and in chapters 18 and 19 where
the title occurs twelve times. Similarly *basileia* (reign, kingdom)
occurs again only twice in 18:36, not now as "the kingdom of
God" but as "my kingdom". John obviously wishes to connect
the theme of Jesus' kingship with the cross where his reign is
supremely manifested, and where the kingdom of God is now
the kingdom of Christ.

It is however by no means obvious to all that the man on the
cross is a king, in spite of the wording of the titulus. It is only
God's action which reveals Jesus' kingship. Nicodemus there-

fore, the representative human being and the representative Jew, will never be able to appreciate God's reign in Jesus except as the result of God's own action. The need of a new birth is expressed in another way in 6:44 – "No-one can come to me unless the Father who sent me draws him", and yet it is the action of Jesus on the cross which makes this possible – "I, if I be lifted up from the earth will draw all people to me" (12:32).

Baptism and new birth

Nicodemus, in regular Johannine manner, misunderstands Jesus. Like the outsiders of Mark 4:11 he cannot grasp Jesus' parabolic language and gives it its literal meaning. For him *anothen* means "again". The elucidation of 3:5 – "*Amen, amen, I tell you unless one is born of water and spirit he cannot enter the kingdom of God*" – is equally unintelligible to Nicodemus. The readers of the gospel, corresponding to the insiders of Mark, know full well the reference which John intends. New birth "of water and spirit" cannot but refer to the baptism already promised in 1:33. Bultmann (1971:138) believed that the words "water and" (*hudatos kai*) were inserted by the ecclesiastical redactor to provide a baptismal reference which was otherwise not intended. The textual evidence clearly shows that they are an authentic part of the text as we have it. De la Potterie (1962) considers the words from a literary point of view and concludes that although they were probably an addition to the source which John used, they were inserted to emphasize more clearly the baptismal reference of the passage. De la Potterie therefore believes that they reflect the already long tradition of Christian baptism, and that John wished to stress both the objective action of baptism and the need of faith, by asserting that the new birth is produced "by the baptism of water and by the Spirit who gives us faith" (1962:440, translated). This view is supported by the phrase "to believe in his name" (1:12; 2:23; 3:18), where the expression of faith is joined to a baptismal allusion.

The theme of new birth symbolized by baptism and all that it stands for is found too in Titus 3:5, where the reference both to "the washing of rebirth" (*loutrou palingenesias*) and to the Holy Spirit is most easily seen as the confirmation of the promise made in the gospels by John the Baptist (Mk 1:8; Mt 3:11; Lk 3:16; Jn 1:33). In none of the gospels is the contrast simply between baptism in water and baptism in the Spirit. Since the word *baptizein* means "to dip" or "to immerse" (cf Mk 7:4; 2 Kg 5:14 LXX) the use of water was always implied. The contrast in the gospels is between baptism in water and baptism in water *and the Spirit* (cf Burge 1987:168). Certainly *baptizein* can be used metaphorically, as in Mark 10:38f, but even there the passage describes the implications of Christian baptism as participation in Christ's death (cf Rom 6:3-6). A similar reference to the new life given in baptism is to be found in 1 Peter 1:3,23, in a letter which clearly refers in one way or another to the privileges and responsibilities of baptism. Baptism, in its connection with the Spirit of God, may be seen as the fulfilment of Ezekiel's prophecy (36:25-27). The allusions elsewhere in the New Testament to this passage (2 Cor 3:3; 1 Th 4:8; Heb 10:22) indicate its pervasive influence. The concept of a new birth is found too in the mystery religions, as is exemplified by Apuleius (*Met* 11:24) who describes the final day of his initiation into the mysteries of Isis as his birthday. The language of new birth in the first century would therefore have been familiar both to readers of the Old Testament and to others. John however attaches the imagery firmly to the person of Jesus.

With such a background the readers of John 3 cannot fail to recognize their own position: they have been baptized, and led by the Spirit they are to see their destiny as no longer being under their own control. Nicodemus cannot understand (v9), for he is still on the outside and has not yet made his act of faith. His doubts provide the context for an address to all the readers of the gospel which is intended to show the relation between their Christian discipleship entered upon in their baptism and God's action in Jesus.

The first person plural used in verse 11 represents not merely the testimony of Jesus but that of his disciples too. The new life is a fact of Christian experience – "we speak of what we know and we bear witness to what we have seen, and you (plural) do not receive our witness". It matters little therefore whether verses 11 to 21 are meant to be assigned to Jesus or to the evangelist, for they both speak with a single voice. So verse 12 reverts to the first person singular: it is the Lord who speaks through the mouth of his witnesses, and he no longer addresses Nicodemus, who has faded into the background, but all who will listen to him. This is shown by the use of the second person plural in verse 12 – "If I have told you of the earthly things (*ta epigeia*) and you do not believe, how will you believe if I tell you of the heavenly things (*ta epourania*)?"

The exact meaning of *ta epigeia* and *ta epourania* must be determined from the context. Neither term is used again in the Johannine writings. Elsewhere in the New Testament *epigeia* refers to what is found on earth (e g 1 Cor 15:40; Phil 3:19), whereas *epourania* denotes what goes on in heaven (e g 1 Cor 15:40; Heb 8:5; 9:23). At first it might look as though Jesus (or John) has already been talking about heavenly matters, with his stress on the birth from above (*anothen*) and the work of the Spirit. If however the allusion in the previous verses is to baptism, the contrast between *epigeia* and *epourania* not only becomes clearer, but it also illustrates John's understanding of baptism. The rite of baptism finds its meaning only in the person of Christ through the work of the Spirit: in itself it has little value, for its purpose is to bring people to faith in Christ and his work. Yet one cannot do without it: to talk of heavenly things (the reality behind the rite) without reference to their earthly manifestations will be of no avail. It is difficult enough, we are assured (Wisdom 9:16), to comprehend what takes place on earth and near at hand "but who has ever traced what happens in heaven (*ta en ouranois*)?" Just as the signs in the gospel are declarations of the glory of God revealed in Jesus and are intended to lead to faith in him (Jn 2:11), so the acts of Christian worship, baptism and eucharist, are declarations of God's work of love in Jesus and are meant to awaken or sustain faith in Christ.

So the enigmatic verse 12 is followed in the next verse by the reference to the Son of Man's ascent to, and descent from, heaven. Only he who has come from heaven (*ouranos*) can tell of heavenly things (*ta epourania*). Heaven and earth meet together in the person of the Son of Man (cf 1:51): in his own person he is the sign of God's action and revelation in the world

(1:18). But the sign is made clear in what he does. Verse 14 therefore refers to his glorification. The lifting up of the brass serpent on the pole by Moses in the wilderness (Num 21:8f) was an important symbol already being interpreted as a symbol of salvation (*sumbolon soterias* – Wisdom 16:6), but not in any magical sense. "For the one who turned to look at it was saved not because of what he saw, but because of Thee the saviour of all" (Wisdom 16:7). Just as the bronze serpent was the "symbol of salvation" effected by God, so baptism is the symbol or sign of the salvation effected by Jesus in his death and resurrection. The elevation of the Son of Man is therefore compared with the elevation of the bronze serpent. Elevation (*hupsoun*) is here used in a double sense, indicating both the act of crucifixion and the exaltation in glory. This is made abundantly clear in 12:32f – "And I, if I am lifted up (*hupsotho*) from the earth will draw all people to myself". This act of God in Christ is perhaps seen to be anticipated in the words of Isaiah concerning the servant of God (52:13): "he will be exalted (*hupsothesetai*) and greatly glorified".

The cross and eternal life

The crucifixion and exaltation of Jesus is the sole foundation for eternal life (*zoe aionios*). This is the first time this phrase has been used in the fourth gospel. The reader has been prepared for it by the references to life (*zoe*) in 1:4. It now appears that "eternal life" is the same as "the kingdom of God". To enter into the kingdom of God is to find eternal life. Origen (Catena *ad loc*: Preuschen 1903:515) comments "Eternal life is not the ordinary kind of life which belongs to other animals too, but it is life which depends on faith and every other virtue". John 3:15 declares that this life is available to those who have faith. The purpose of the incarnation is therefore described more fully in 3:16-21. From God's side his gracious act of love is shown in Christ, sent to be the saviour of the world (3:17; cf 4:42): but this becomes real when people accept it in faith. This is indicated especially in the act of baptism, to which verse 18 alludes – "the one who does not believe has already been judged because he has not believed (*me pepisteuken*) in the name (*eis to onoma*) of the only son of God". This verse develops the thought of verses 15 and 16. The use of the perfect tense (*pepisteuken*) is to be noted. Louw (1967) argues that the true semantic value of the perfect is to be found in the stress on the content of the verb rather than on its temporal aspect. In this case therefore the stress is on the need of faith. But the contrast between the present ("the one who does not believe") and the perfect helps to indicate that faith had been expressed in the past, in the act of baptism. The irregular use of the negative *me* instead of the usual *ou* is presumably due to its use, quite regularly, with the participle in the same verse (*ho me pisteuon*) so as to stress that the grounds for the judgement are simply the refusal to believe and so to accept Jesus as the saviour. The phrase "in(to) the name" recalls the baptismal formula (Mt 28:19; Ac 8:16; 19:5; 1 Cor 1:13,15), which occurs also elsewhere in slightly different forms (*epi to onomati* Ac 2:38; *en to onomati* Ac 10:48; 1 Cor 6:11).

The whole of the fourth gospel asserts the centrality of Jesus for life and faith. He is the light of the world, and to come to him is to find light (3:21). It is not therefore surprising that in later periods those who were in the last stages of preparation for baptism were called "those who are being enlightened" (*hoi photizomenoi*) and the baptized were called "the enlightened ones" (*hoi photisthentes*). It is not unlikely that a similar terminology was being used for the baptized in the time of the New Testament writings, as is suggested especially by Ephesians 1:18; 5:8,14; Colossians 1:12; 1 Thessalonians 5:5; 2 Timothy 1:10; Hebrews 6:4; 10:32. All these texts refer to the light brought by Christ to those who have committed themselves to him, so that "he who comes to the light" (Jn 3:21) would be a good description of the one who expresses faith in Christ in baptism. This may be confirmed by the use of the Hebraic phrase "doing the truth" in verse 21, which in the Old Testament refers especially to the observance of the Torah, as is shown especially in Tobit 4:5-6:

> ... child, remember the Lord our God: do not willingly transgress his commandments. Follow righteousness all the days of your life, and do not go into the way of injustice. Because as long as you do the truth you will

prosper in your works ...

In Ezekiel 18:9 "to do the truth" is the summary of walking in the commandments of God. In the gospel Jesus takes the place of the Torah as the guide and norm for a true life, as is shown quite clearly in 1 John 1:6 – "If we should say that we have fellowship with him and yet walk in the darkness, we are liars and are not doing the truth". Baptism into the name of Christ brings people into fellowship (*koinonia*) with him, and this fellowship is demonstrated by the nature and quality of their lives.

The pericope ends (3:22-30) with an explicit reference to baptism, contrasting that of John the Baptist with that of Jesus. This contrast not only emphasizes the role of John as witness to Jesus, but also helps the readers of the gospel to interpret all that has gone before in the light of their own baptism. Baptism is a gift from God (3:27), and when it has been received the believer is involved in a new life of commitment to Christ. John 3:22 and 26 alone in the New Testament refer to Jesus as himself baptizing others, even though this appears to be contradicted by 4:2. It would be easy to suggest that 4:2 is a scribal note to show that since Christian baptism was always connected with the death and resurrection of Jesus, it was impossible that Jesus himself could have practised baptism. There is however no textual evidence for the omission of 4:2, and this verse should be interpreted together with 3:22,26. Just as 3:11 seems to mean that Christian disciples share with Jesus the task of bearing witness to him, so the reader of the gospel is helped to recall that in his own baptism, performed by a Christian disciple, the true minister was Jesus himself, the risen Lord. (Smith 1982:94, it may be noted in passing, believes that the original Aramaic source of 3:22 read "Jesus baptized nobody but his disciples". But this view is adopted to suit his own theories.)

Further reasons for considering John 3 as referring to baptism are provided in verses 31 to 36. The language of verse 31 harks back to the beginning of the dialogue with Nicodemus: "the one who comes from above" (*anothen*) refers primarily to Jesus, but the phrase refers too to everyone who has heard the Lord and expressed faith in him in baptism. The true origin of the disciple, as of Jesus, is found in God. This theme appears in various forms throughout the fourth gospel. In 1:12-13 "those who believe in his name" are contrasted with those born "of blood and of the will of the flesh" (*ex haimaton, ek thelematos sarkos*), and are said to be born "of God" (*ek theou*). In 8:23 Jesus himself is described as claiming to be from above (*ek ton ano*) whereas the unbelieving Jews are said to be from below (*ek ton kato*) and from the world (*ek tou kosmou*). In 17:14,16 both Jesus and his disciples are those who do not derive their being from the world. In every case the same preposition (*ek*) is used, indicating source or origin. John 3:31 therefore resumes the theme which has already been expounded in verses 2 to 8, and which forms the context for understanding the whole chapter. But since verses 31 to 36 occur between two references to baptism (vv23-26 and 4:1-2) the baptismal context of the whole chapter is confirmed.

The whole discussion is however closely connected to Jesus and his work, and its purpose is to strengthen the readers of the gospel in their commitment to Jesus the Lord as they are led to see ever deeper implications of their baptism, which is not an outward rite so much as the establishment of a new relationship between the believer and God. In accepting baptism the believer accepts God's seal as showing that he or she belongs to God. The verb "to seal" (*sphragizein*) even in New Testament times seems often to refer to baptism, as can be seen from 2 Corinthians 1:22 and Ephesians 1:13; 4:30, if not from John 6:27 which may well be a reference to the baptism of Jesus. The use of the same verb in 3:33 serves to show that acceptance of the testimony given to Jesus involves a commitment on the part of the believer too, who sets his seal to the truth of God as declared in Jesus. God seals the believer with the Holy Spirit and marks him out as his own (Eph 1:13f). But the candidate sets his seal too to the covenant made by God, just as the Israelites promised to obey God's words spoken by Moses (Ex 24:7). This is presumably the context of Revelation 7:3-8, which refers back to Ezekiel 9:2-6, where the mark is the letter *taw*, written in old Hebrew in the form of a cross. Revelation refers to those who have been baptized into the death of Christ (Rom 6:3), who bear his name (Ac 9:15) and who are called to share in the victory of Christ by their loyalty and faithfulness to him (Rev 2:7; 21:7). Perhaps the later practice of marking candidates for baptism with the sign of the cross on their foreheads was already being followed in New Testament times.

John 3:34-36 refers to the work of God – Father, Son and Holy Spirit. Rightly so, for although we may not try to find any developed trinitarian theology in the gospels, baptism certainly refers to the work of the Father, the Son and the Spirit (cf Mt 28:19), and indicates the entrance into the new life (*zoe aionios*, v36) which is fellowship with the Father and the Son in the Spirit. From the human side entrance into this new life requires obedience to God. It is therefore probable that *apeithon* in verse 36b should have its usual meaning "disobey", as in most modern versions, though the AV renders it by "believeth not".

John 4 in relation to John 3

Chapter 3 started with Nicodemus "a ruler of the Jews", and it ends with the assertion that eternal life, life of the new age, is dependent upon faith in Jesus the Son of the Father. Nicodemus' question (if question it is) is answered in two stages. First of all there is a reference to a new birth by water and the Spirit, with a clear allusion to baptism. This is what is meant by speaking of earthly things (*ta epigeia* – v12). Then follows the explanation that eternal life and salvation result from the love of God in sending his only Son to be exalted on the cross (cf 1 Jn 4:9). The two stages are closely connected: baptism is the outward sign, but its meaning is found only in the cross of Christ. The conversation with Nicodemus describes the journey which the true Israelite, already anticipated in Nathanael (1:47-51), ought to be making if he is to find God's kingdom. It is therefore fitting that Nicodemus is present at the cross (19:39) where he has come to find eternal life in the death of Jesus. The story of the meeting with Nicodemus expresses in another way the message of Cana of Galilee (2:1-11) and the cleansing of the Temple (2:13-22): the fulfilment of Israel's hopes, as expressed in the Old Testament and in their liturgy, is found in the death of Jesus and in his resurrection and continued life through the

Spirit.

Chapter 4 continues with a similar theme: a reminder of baptismal connotations is provided in verses 1 and 2. The pericope as a whole (4:1-42) shows the superiority of the new dispensation over the old. Jacob's well certainly provided sustenance to the Israelites (v12), but the true sustenance for God's people is found only in Jesus. Although Jacob's gift to his son included a spring (*pege* v6), for the Samaritan woman it was a cistern (*phrear* vv11-12). The background here is to be found in Jeremiah 2:13, where the people are described as having forsaken YHWH who is the spring (*pege*) of life, and as having dug for themselves cisterns (Heb *bo'rôt*, Gk *lakkoi*) which cannot hold water, where *bo'r* is contrasted with *maqôr* (fountain). Once again Jesus is shown as fulfilling the promises of the Old Testament: he is the source of the living water, which in Jeremiah is the description of YHWH. Water not only recalls Christian baptism: it is also the symbol of the Spirit, as 7:38-39 makes clear. The "spring of water leaping up into eternal life" (v14) is therefore to be seen as referring to the gift of the Spirit which the risen Christ will give (16:7). In chapter 4 then there recur the themes of the previous chapters, and especially those found in chapter 3. Although there are the references to the Spirit, the giver of the water of life is Jesus himself. The uninitiated may well understand "living water" (*hudor zon*) in its usual sense to refer merely to running water. But Christians will remember what has already been said about water and the Spirit and will understand the allusions to baptism without much difficulty, for it is in baptism that they have received the gift of the water of life. Once again, however, it is not baptism in itself which is important, but its meaning, which is now spelt out in 4:16-42.

The command to the woman in verse 16 "Go and call your husband" is properly to be understood not as a reference to her personal marital life, but as referring to her commitment to the right God. Isaiah 54:5 describes Israel's true husband (your *ba'al*) as YHWH, in contrast to the other *baals* to whom the Israelites so frequently gave their allegiance. This constant theme of the Old Testament is expressed particularly vividly in Ezekiel 16. The address to the woman of Samaria in these words (v16) sets the stage for a new scene in the drama. The first part of the story (as with the narrative of Nicodemus) describes the fulfilment of the Old Testament prophecies in Jesus, with allusions to the action by which people are made his disciples. The second part (vv16-42, and especially vv16-26) fixes the reader's attention on Jesus as the true source of life and the revealer of YHWH. Jesus' comment therefore – "You have had five husbands, and the one you now have is not your husband" (v18) – clearly refers to the false gods mentioned in 2 Kings 17:30f, which were apparently considered to be five in number (Jos *Ant* 9:288-290) even though seven names are mentioned in 2 Kings 17. The woman, representing the Samaritans, does not have a husband, because (as is made clear in v22) the true worship of YHWH is found only among the Jews, and the Samaritans' worship is an impure worship (Marsh 1968:215f). Salvation comes from the Jews: the faith and worship of the Christian church therefore is not a rejection of the treasures of Judaism, but the fulfilment in which they find their true value. So the worship at Jerusalem, the centre of Israelite devotion, will give place to the worship which is centred on Jesus, and which is in spirit and truth (vv23f), where spirit presumably refers to the Holy Spirit to whom allusion has been made in the preceding verses. Jesus' self-disclosure in verse 26 is the climax, and the nature of his messiahship is explained in the rest of the gospel. Worship in spirit and truth means worship centred upon Jesus, the truth (14:6) to whom the Spirit continually bears witness (14:26).

Many themes can no doubt be traced as running through the narrative of Jesus and the Samaritan woman, and the attentive reader will be able to pick up all sorts of allusions. Not only are there the references to the Old Testament: there is also a series of allusions to the Passion Narrative. This is just what we should expect if we are to see the connection between the rite of baptism and the person and work of Jesus. The following points may be specially noted.

Verse 6 draws attention to Jacob's well: the well signifies the Torah, as Lyonnet (1974:225) indicates with references from Qumran (CD 6:4) and from the *Mekilta*. The Greek version of Proverbs 4:20-22 seems to identify God's words (*logoi*) with the Israelites' springs (*pegai*) in which life is to be found. Certainly the Torah was meant to be the source of life (Rom 7:10), but it is only in Jesus, the fulfilment of the Torah, that the true source of life is to be found. He is the true Word of God, the true Torah: but the fulfilment which he brings is to be seen not merely in his person, who he is, but in his work, what he has done. John's audience is alerted to this in various ways. "Jesus, wearied (*kekopiakos*) from his journeying (*hodoiporias*), sat as he was (*houtos*) at the well: it was about mid-day (*hora en hos hekte*)." The verb *kopian* can mean either "to labour" or "to grow weary". In the former sense it is used particularly to refer to the work of Christian evangelists and missionaries (e g Ac 20:35; Rom 16:12). It is used twice with this meaning in John 4:38, the only other occurrence of the word in the fourth gospel. The noun *kopos*, which also occurs in verse 38, is used in Hermas *Sim* 5:6:2 to describe the work of salvation effected by Jesus. It is likely therefore that the verb in 4:6 (having laboured) connotes the work of Christ, and this possibility is strengthened by the following clause – "it was about mid-day" – a clause which recurs only in 19:14 in the course of the Passion Narrative.

Once the reader has been alerted to possible allusions to the passion of Christ other clues are provided. In verse 7 "Give me a drink" corresponds to "I thirst" in 19:28. This word is uttered by Jesus immediately before he died on the cross with the word "It is accomplished" (*tetelestai*), after which "he handed over the spirit" (*paredoken to pneuma* – 19:30), which can simply mean that he died, but can also mean that it was in and through his death that he gave the Spirit to those who would commit themselves to him. In 4:7 the request for a drink is followed by the promise of the perennial spring of water of life which the Lord will give, water being a common symbol for the Spirit (Jn 7:38-39).

The conversation with the woman carries on to mention the coming of an hour when the nature of worship will be changed (v21). The clause is repeated in verse 23 when it is reinforced by the addition "and is now here". Already the glorification of Jesus on the cross is anticipated. In the fourth gospel, as has been mentioned earlier, the hour is especially the hour of the glorification of Jesus on the cross. Later in the narrative (v34) Jesus talks of his food as "to do the work of the one who sent me and to finish his work", where the verb "to finish" (*teleioun*) is used especially of the work of Jesus on the cross (17:4), and the related words *telos*, *telein*, are used with a similar reference (13:1; 19:30). So Jesus' words to his disciples in 4:38 have a twofold meaning: on the one hand the disciples are building upon the work and witness of the people of the Old Testament, and on the other the real work (*kopos*) into which they have entered is Christ's work completed on the cross.

Chapter 4 therefore is rich in allusions not only to Christian baptism as the source of life, but also to the person and work of Jesus who alone can give meaning through his death on the cross to the rite of baptism. Such a view of the passage means that the hearers or readers of the gospel are aware of the ending of the gospel when listening to the beginning. Since the gospels were meant to be read over and over again, in such a context words and phrases would continually be found to have a deeper meaning than at first appeared. Like all great literature, the meaning of the gospels can never be exhausted, and their interpretation can never be finally and definitively determined. To make the meaning of God's act in Christ vivid and relevant John continually alluded to the acts of Christian worship with which his audience was familiar and the meaning of which was to be found always in Christ and his work. For the same reason a reading from the gospels has always formed part of every eucharistic celebration from the earliest times, since the ritual act and the words of the gospel interpret each other.

4

Jesus, the bread of life: John 6

Panem nostrum supersubstantialem da nobis hodie.
(Give us today our supernatural bread)

The Vulgate of Matthew 6:11

Faith and sacrament

The earlier chapters of the gospel (2:1-11,13-22; 3:1-21; 4:4-42,46-54) provide vivid examples of the new life brought by Jesus. The acceptance of this new life depends on faith in Jesus, which means obedience to his commands (1:12; 3:36). New life needs to be sustained in order that it might grow and develop, and any religious community therefore needs to have ways in which its corporate faith may be continually renewed and repeatedly confessed. However important the personal expression of faith may be – and John, as we have already seen and shall see again, does not wish to deny this – faith always involves entrance into a community which expresses its corporate faith in its liturgical observances, where each member supports, and is supported by, others who share the same faith and hope. Chapter 6 describes the ground of this corporate faith, with constant allusions and references to the eucharist as the regular expression of the community's faith in Jesus and his love. Faith and the sacrament, as Feuillet (1985:104) observes, are in perfect harmony with each other, for the life-giving communion with Christ which is inaugurated by faith finds its true consummation in the sacrament.

There is no doubt that the miraculous feeding of the multitudes, recorded twice in Mark and Matthew, and once in both Luke and John, made a lasting impression on all who experienced or recounted it. This is scarcely surprising, since it is narrated in all the gospels in a way which could not fail to remind the readers of the events at the Last Supper and the institution of the eucharist.

We may note the clear allusions in Mark 6:41 – "he took (*labon*) the bread, he looked up to heaven (the attitude of prayer), he said the blessing (*eulogesen*), he broke (*kateklasen*) the loaves and gave (*edidou*) them to his disciples that they might distribute them to the people, and after they were satisfied they took up twelve baskets of broken pieces (*klasmata*)". Mark 8:6, at the feeding of the four thousand, displays a similar order – "he took (*labon*) the seven loaves, and after saying the blessing (*eucharistesas*), he broke (*eklasen*) them and gave (*edidou*) them to his disciples that they might distribute them". The account of the Last Supper (Mk 14:22) tells how Jesus took (*labon*) bread, said the blessing (*eulogesas*), broke (*eklasen*) the bread and gave (*edoken*) it to them. Here we have the same words in the same order (except that the simple *eklasen* is used instead of the compound *kateklasen* in 6:41). Audet believed (1958:377-398) that the original Aramaic behind both *eucharistein* (give thanks) and *eulogein* (bless) referred to the Jewish prayer of *berakah* in which God is praised and blessed for his marvellous works in creation and redemption. Talley however argues (1976) that *berakah* is not the same as *eucharistia*. The Christian liturgy, in giving special prominence to to the idea of thanksgiving, shows both the similarity of Christian forms of worship to Jewish forms and the difference between them. Mark was right to use *eulogein* (bless) for the bread at the start of the meal (Mk 14:22) and *eucharistein* (give thanks) over the wine at the conclusion of the meal (14:23), in thanksgiving to God for his act of redemption in Christ. The use of both words by Mark in each of the accounts of the miraculous feeding helps to relate these accounts to the Last Supper and to the church's eucharist. In addition, *klasma* (Mk 6:43) seems to have been used as the technical term for the broken bread of the eucharist (Did 9:3-4). Mark wrote his gospel with great skill, and it may well be that the accounts of the feeding of the multitude are duplicated, with the same order of actions at the Last Supper and at the Christian eucharist, in order to emphasize the way in which the Lord continues to feed his people miraculously in the eucharist. It could indeed be argued that Mark's account of Jesus' actions at the miraculous feedings simply described what any pious Jew would do before a meal. In view, however, of the meaning assigned to Jesus' actions and words at the Last Supper (Mk 14:22-25), an allusion to the eucharist seems inevitable.

If this is true of Mark's gospel, we can expect it all the more in the fourth gospel, where we should bear in mind the prayer of Origen as he sets out to expound the gospel's meaning – "Let us now ask God to work with us through Christ in the Holy Spirit to unfold the mystical meaning which is stored up in the words and phrases" (*Comm in ev Ioh* 1:15:89; Preuschen 1903:19). Burge (1987:178) believes that "a primary reference to the eucharist in 6:1-15 is tenuous at best". This is surprising in view of his belief that in verses 52 to 58 the use of *haima* (blood) "makes the eucharistic application inescapable" (1987:182). Certainly the miracle is not narrated as an allegory of the eucharist, but John's narrative is influenced by the eucharist and therefore is written in a way which helps the readers or hearers of the gospel to recognize the way in which the Lord continues to feed his people miraculously.

Is chapter 6 misplaced?

In attempting to discover the eucharistic references *and* theology in John 6 we must begin with the context. It is well known that chapter 6 appears to interrupt the logical order of events recorded in chapters 5 and 7. Bultmann's reconstruction of the original order (1971:209) makes good sense, but like all attempts to change the order it suffers from the disadvantage that there is no textual evidence to support any such dislocation. Whatever the original order may have been, we are obliged to take the text as it is and to see if there is any good reason for it, remembering that the fourth gospel is concerned especially to explain the meaning of Jesus and his acts rather than to relate his history.

Chapter 4 ends with the healing of the nobleman's son – a dramatic example of Jesus' ability to give life. Its importance is stressed by its description as the second sign of Jesus (v54), and it is related to 2:1-11 by the reference to Cana. Chapter 5 brings Jesus back to Jerusalem, at the time of the celebration of a feast. The chapter resumes previous themes – healing by the word of Jesus, and fulfilment of the Old Testament. It also provides the fullest treatment so far of the authority and person of Jesus.

The healing of 5:2-9 seems to be John's version of the incident recorded in Mark 2:1-12, but in spite of similarities it is very different. John 5:2 refers to a pool (*kolumbethra*) at the sheep-gate (*probatike*) or (as some manuscripts and Origen have it) to the sheep-pool. Jeremias, after a careful survey of the archaeological and linguistic evidence, concludes (1949:6) that the correct translation should be: "There is in Jerusalem at the sheep-pool (a place) called in Aramaic Bethesda, with five porticoes." Origen (Catena *ad loc*: Preuschen 1903:532-533) says that the name was derived from the fact that the sheep for sacrifice were assembled there, and the entrails of the victims were washed in the pool. This was reputed to give healing property to the water. If the name refers to the gate (cf Neh 3:1,32; 12:39) it would be connected with the gate by which sheep were brought into the city for sacrifice at the Temple. In either case an allusion to Jesus as the true sacrifice would not be difficult to find, especially in view of 10:7 ("I am the door of the sheep") and 10:15 ("I lay down my life for the sheep, *probata*").

The word for pool (*kolumbethra*) occurs in the New Testament only in John 5:2,7 and 9:7. It has the general meaning of pool, but was used in later Christian literature to refer in one way or another exclusively to the baptismal font (Lampe 1961:766). In both instances in John it is used in a narrative which describes the giving of new life. In chapter 5 the cripple is not put into the pool; he is healed simply by the word of Jesus. As the healing occurred on the Sabbath (v9), it provided the occasion for the discussion of Jesus' authority and his relation to the Father. He is described as the one through whom God gives life (vv21,24-26). The importance of the statements is indicated by the three-fold use of the double *amen* (vv19,24,25), a feature which is found too in 3:3,5,11; 6:26,32,47,53; 9:34,51,58 and 13:16,20,21. All the chapters in which this feature occurs are of special importance in the disclosure of the nature and work of Christ.

John 5 therefore starts with the account of the cripple who is healed by the word of Christ, and continues from verse 17 with an explanation of the work of Christ. Verse 17 uses the introductory word *apekrinato* (he answered). This middle form of the verb is not often used in the New Testament and seems to indicate a particularly solemn utterance (Moulton & Milligan 1914-1929:64), shown especially in the papyri. Such a use is found in John only in 5:17-19 and, according to some manuscripts, in 12:23. (A specially good example occurs in Acts 3:12.) The argument of Jesus is that his Father has been working up till now, that is up to the Sabbath, which is observed as a commemoration (Ex 20:8 – "Remember (*zakor*) the sabbath day") of God's work of creation, and which was recognized as the sign (*'ôt*) of God's perpetual covenant (*berît*) with Israel (Ex 31:12-17). Jesus claims therefore to be carrying on God's work, and so introducing the new covenant and the new age, symbolized by the eighth day, to which a clear allusion is found later in 7:22-23. The observance of the Sabbath was one of the most important ways in which Israel was continually reminded that they were a nation holy to the Lord, God's own people. To break the Sabbath commandment blurred the distinction between Israel and other nations (gentiles, *ta ethne*). The argument therefore proceeds to show how the work of God in passing judgement and giving life has been committed to the Son in such a way that the one who does not honour the Son does not honour the Father.

The chapter concludes (vv31-47) with a detailed argument of the way in which the work of Jesus has received witness not only from John the Baptist and Jesus' own works, but also from the Old Testament, and especially from Moses. It is as though all the allusions to the Old Testament in the previous chapters have been explicated theologically in these verses. Verse 38 is especially instructive: the Jews cannot believe because "you do not have his (the Father's) word abiding in you, because you do not believe the one whom he has sent", where "the word" (*logos*) should be taken to refer both to scripture and to Jesus as the incarnate fulfilment of scripture.

In view of this long discussion of the relation between Jesus Christ and the scriptures it would not be surprising to find in the sign which gave rise to it allusions to the Old Testament. Verse 1, with its reference to "a feast of the Jews" prepares the way. Verse 2, as has already been noted, refers either to the sheep-gate or the sheep-pool, with an allusion to the sacrifices in the Temple. (The use of *probata* to describe the sacrificial victims is confirmed by Jn 2:14-15, and by Is 53:7 and Ps 44:22 = Ps 43:23 LXX, quoted in Ac 8:32 and Rom 8:36 respectively.)

The apparently far-fetched interpretation of Augustine therefore (Hoskyns 1947:264) which saw in the five porticoes (*stoai*) a symbol of the books of the Pentateuch, the Torah, which was unable to bring healing, may not be entirely ruled out. Barrett (1978:253) seems unduly harsh in implying that such symbolism is too crude for John. The fact that the double pool near the church of St Anna seems to have had five porticoes does not necessarily exclude a symbolic interpretation, but is perhaps rather the foundation for it. The sick folk of verse 4 – "sick, blind, lame, paralysed (*xeroi*)" – presumably recall Isaiah 35:5-6, a messianic passage used by Matthew (11:5) and Luke (7:22) to indicate the coming of the Messiah in Jesus, the bringer of health and salvation: "Then the eyes of the blind will be opened and the ears of the deaf will hear. Then will the lame man leap like a deer and the tongue of those who can scarcely talk (LXX *mogilaloi*) will speak clearly." In John 5:4 the Western text (D, *it*) adds the word *paralutikoi* (paralysed), perhaps to bring it closer to Isaiah, which refers to "feeble hands and paralysed (*paralelumena*) knees" (35:3). So the period of thirty-eight years during which the cripple lay sick should not be taken either as an arbitrary figure or as a historically accurate statement, in spite of the doubts of Hoskyns (1947:265) and Barrett (1978:253). This period of time is mentioned in the Old Testament only in Deuteronomy 2:14, describing the wanderings of the Israelites in the wilderness and the failure of a whole generation to reach the promised land. Since John expects his readers to know the Old Testament, the number is unlikely to be a mere coincidence.

If this is so, then the man is representative of the Jews waiting for salvation, and finding it only by the word of Jesus who, unlike other men who refuse, or are unable, to help the cripple, gives him health (cf Haenchen 1984a:255). Any allusion to baptism which may be implied by the word *kolumbethra* is firmly in the background, the whole stress being on the person and work of Jesus, the fulfilment of the Old Testament promises. The following verses (vv10-47) explain the relation between the work of Jesus and the words of Moses which bear witness to him, so that belief in the words of Moses should issue in faith in Jesus.

The same theme of faith and disbelief is resumed with the confession of Peter at the end of chapter 6 (vv68-69) after which Jesus stayed in Galilee (7:1), and then went up to Jerusalem for the feast of Tabernacles (7:2,10), where the Jews wondered who he was. Some were prepared to call him a good man, whereas others thought that he was misleading the people (7:12). Jesus' teaching in the Temple evoked the wonder of the Jews (7:15), as a result of which Jesus developed the answer which he gave the Jews in 5:19-47. Circumcision (7:22) was given by Moses in order that a man may be made whole. So important was the law of circumcision that it took precedence over the law of the Sabbath (Barrett 1978:320, who provides the rabbinic references). Now, the eighth day was especially symbolic of the new creation, and was particularly associated with baptism, since the eighth day was the day of the resurrection of Jesus, the beginning of the new creation, or, as the *Epistle of Barnabas* has it, "the beginning of another world" (15:8-9). Every Sunday, the first day and the eighth day, commemorates the end of the old and the beginning of the new. The stress in the fourth gospel is on the wholeness of life brought by Jesus through his death and resurrection, and anticipated by the words of Moses and the rite of circumcision. But though there is no direct reference to baptism, Christians would know that it was their baptism which marked their new creation, and no doubt would have seen baptism as having a similar meaning to circumcision (cf Col 2:11), by which they became a new creation (2 Cor 5:17) in Jesus Christ as God's people.

The feeding of the multitude

Between chapters 5 and 7 there occurs the narrative of the feeding of the multitude and the subsequent discourse. The hearers of the gospel have listened to the theological argument of 5:17-47 to which, as Lightfoot notes (1960:141), John attaches great importance. John, like any good preacher, knows that there is a limit to be placed on such discursive argument. So he returns to narrative in 6:1, telling the well-known story of the miraculous feeding in such a way that it provides the opening for a discourse on the central act of the church's worship, the eucharist. The story reflects Old Testament narratives. Ruddick (1968:340-341), following John Chrysostom (*Hom in ev Ioh* 42:2), connects it with Genesis 22:1-14, and argues that the differences in John's account from that of the synoptics can all be accounted for by reference to this passage from Genesis. The feeding thus "looks forward to Jesus giving his own body on the cross and in the sacrificial banquet of the eucharist, and backward ... to Abraham ...". His suggestion that Genesis 22:1-14 was the reading from the synagogue which John 6:1-14 was intended to match, though lacking any firm basis for the first century, would demonstrate very clearly the function of the liturgy in making the connection between the message of the Old Testament and its fulfilment in Christ. Daube (1973:27-51) on the other hand finds the Old Testament background in the book of Ruth, which the Rabbis interpreted with reference to the messianic age and eschatological food. He quotes *Bab Shab* 113b "she did eat – *in this world* – and was filled – *for the day of the Messiah* – and left thereof – *for the Age to come*". Brown (1966:233) notes several similarities between John 6:1-15 and the account in Numbers 11 of the feeding of the Israelites with manna and quails.

John 6 therefore provides a good illustration of the argument of 5:31-47. All that was foreshadowed in the Old Testament finds its fulfilment in Jesus. This is worked out in great detail by Borgen (1965:61-65,72-97) who considers John's use of midrashic exegesis of the Old Testament to be in line with that of Philo and the rabbinic commentary, the *Mekilta*, on Exodus. The parallels with Philo are specially noteworthy as showing the prevalence of this form of Jewish exegesis in the first century AD. The difference in John's exegesis is that it is entirely controlled by his experience and understanding of Jesus and his work.

John's allusions, however, are not confined to the Old Testament, but refer also to the eucharist, the supreme Christian example of miraculous feeding. So the reference to the Passover (v4) is made not so much to indicate the date as to set the context of the event, as in 2:13, 11:55 and 13:1. The meaning of the Passover, as the second century homily of Melito makes clear (Lohse:1958), is fulfilled in the passion and resurrection of Christ, and it is to this that the acts of Christian worship refer, so that every mention of the *Pascha* (Passover) reminds the Christian of the eucharist (cf Haenchen 1984a:271). But for Melito, as for John, the real "mystery of the *Pascha*" is not the eucharist, but Christ himself (Lohse 1958: lines 387-388).

The action of Jesus "lifting up his eyes" (v5) has a liturgical ring about it (cf 11:41, 17:1), and recalls the saying in John 4:35, "Lift up your eyes and see the lands that they are ripe for harvest". There the reference seems to be to the missionary opportunity facing the church (Hoskyns 1947:246). Here on the other hand Jesus lifts up his eyes and sees the large crowds coming to him, since he, now risen and ascended, John would have us understand, draws people to himself as surely as he did in his incarnate life.

The act of the lad (*paidarion*, cf 2 Kg 4:38,41 LXX) may be meant to recall the offertory at the eucharist. Such an interpretation would draw attention to Brown's warning against concluding that because a passage can be interpreted sacramentally, this was the evangelist's intention (1966:cxii). In view of other features in the narrative, however, it may well be that the lad's action not only alludes to the action of Elisha in providing food for one hundred men (2 Kg 4:42-44), but also reminds disciples of the way in which their contributions to the common feast are miraculously transformed. Certainly Jesus took the loaves (*tous artous*), gave thanks and distributed them to the disciples. Here are three of the four eucharistic actions described by Mark. Early scribes seem to have understood this to refer to the eucharist, as is shown by the many manuscripts which read "after giving thanks he distributed the loaves to his disciples, and the disciples distributed them to those who were sitting down". This would reflect the pattern of the eucharist as found in the second century (Justin *Apol* 1:65), and it is likely that the scribal addition was due more to liturgical influence than to assimilation to the accounts in the synoptic gospels. Interestingly, in the account of the miraculous feedings, the word "distribute" (*diadidonai*) is used only by John. A similar phrase is used in Justin's account of the eucharist – "distribution (*diadosis*) is made to each" (*Apol* 1:67).

In John's account there is no reference to the action of breaking, but he not only uses the term *klasmata* (broken pieces) in verses 11 and 12, used elsewhere in the New Testament only in the accounts of the miraculous feedings, he also uses the word *sunagein* (gather together), which is one of the technical descriptions of the meeting of Christians for worship (e g 1 Cor 5:4; Rev 19:17; Justin *Apol* 1:65). In Didache 9:4, in what appears to be the eucharistic prayer, occurs the petition "As this broken bread (*klasma*) has been scattered upon the mountains and when gathered together (*sunachthen*) became one, so let your church be gathered together (*sunachtheto*) from the ends of the world into your kingdom". The number twelve occurs in the fourth gospel only in chapter 6 (vv13,67,70,71) and in 20:24, apart from its use in a different context in 11:9. Its use in chapter 6 may be to suggest the fullness of the Christian assembly (cf Rev 21:14), in which case there is a further similarity between John's account of the miraculous feeding and the language of Didache.

The stress in John's account is especially on the quantity of bread remaining. Daube (1973:38) goes so far as to say that "the supreme miracle ... is ... exclusively in the bread remaining – or probably ... in all the bread remaining", and he draws particular attention to the fact that "the gathering of the remains alone is reported in a main clause". There is little doubt that John wishes his readers to recognize that the food which Jesus gives is an inexhaustible supply leading to eternal life (*zoe aionios*), as the subsequent discourse makes clear.

If the discourse is meant to interpret the meaning of the miraculous feeding, one could expect the miracle to be related in suggestive terms. In spite of allusions already mentioned, the lack of any reference to wine or to the cup has led many to believe that the accounts in John and the synoptics were not intended to allude to the eucharist. Here we note the import- ance of the symbolism of the fish. Goodenough (1965:98-101) adduces evidence to suggest that for the Jews fish were an important symbol, and possibly formed part of ritualistic meals. Certainly the Rabbis thought of themselves as "little fishes living in the water of Torah, and sure to perish if they tried to escape from it". Goodenough has good reason for believing that Ter- tullian's famous comment (*Bapt* 1) that "we little fishes, just as Jesus Christ is our great fish (*ichthus*), are born in water, and we shall be safe only by remaining in the water" is an inappro- priate christianizing of the Jewish symbolism. Goodenough also refers to Jewish legends which told how the Israelites in the wilderness received not only water from the rock which Moses struck but also fat fishes to eat. In view of the later Talmudic belief that Pisces, the sign of the zodiac, was a symbol of the age of the Messiah, and in view of the frequent occurrence of fish in early Jewish art, it is very likely that the Christian use of the symbol of fish, especially with reference to the eucharist, as the evidence of the catacombs makes clear, was another way of describing the fulfilment of Jewish messianic hopes in Jesus.

The use of fish in the miraculous feedings confirms the general testimony of the gospels that Jesus is himself the fulfilment of Old Testament hopes, while the language of the feeding contin- ually alludes to the eucharist as the liturgical action in which this fulfilment is expressed. The connection of the sign with the discourse which follows is marked by the use of *bibroskein* (feed) in verse 13 and *brosis* (food) in verses 27 and 55. The verb is not found elsewhere in the New Testament, and the noun *brosis* is used in the fourth gospel always with reference to Jesus and his work.

The sign naturally evokes the statement (6:14) that Jesus must be the promised prophet, with a reference presumably to Deuteronomy 18:15, a text which is explicitly cited in Acts 3:22 and 7:37. John, however, uses the text to show that Jesus is raised up as a prophet not only for Israel but for the world. The following verse is an example of Johannine irony, showing the people's ignorance both of the identity of Jesus and of the true meaning of kingship. They want to make Jesus king, in their sense of kingship, when in fact Jesus is already king by God's grace (1:49). Ironically, however, they eventually achieve their purpose when they hand Jesus over to the chief priests and to Pilate (19:14,19).

The narrative of the walking on the water which follows seems to have been closely connected in tradition with the miraculous feeding (cf Mk 6:45-52). It is intended to explain the person of Jesus, and to show that he is not simply the prophet, nor an earthly king, but the one who, like God himself, calms the storm and brings the disciples to their destination (v21; cf Ps 107:28-30). So his words to the disciples (v20) "I am (*ego eimi*); do not fear", recall the divine name of Exodus, to which John certainly refers in 8:58. It is of interest to note that the same words are used in the parallel passages of Mark 6:50 and Matthew 14:27, as though the meaning of the preceding miracle is to be found in the person of Jesus – just as the meaning of the church's worship at the eucharist is found in Jesus and his work. If this is John's intention it must be noted that the words *ego eimi* are deliberately ambiguous, as can be seen from 9:9 where the healed blind man uses the same words with the meaning "I am he". They are therefore intelligible only to those who have ears to hear. The words, like the signs, demand the act of faith in Jesus before they can take on their true meaning.

The identity of Jesus in chapters 5 to 8 is continually being more clearly revealed, and the climax is reached in 8:58. The rest of chapter 6 prepares the way by relating the historical person of Jesus to the acts of Christian worship, and it looks as though the clause "when the Lord had given thanks" (*eucharistesantos tou kuriou*) in verse 23 is meant to draw attention to this interpretation. The genuineness of these words is called into question by their omission in some examples of the Western text (D 091 *pc* a e sy[s,c]) and by the unusual use of *kurios* (Lord) as a description of Jesus in narrative before the resurrection, found elsewhere only at 4:1 (where many mss read "Jesus") and at 11:2, though it occurs nine times in chapters 20 and 21. It may however be deliberately used here to allude to the presence of the risen Lord with his disciples in their worship. This would explain its use too in the story of the raising of Lazarus.

The discourse on the bread of life

The discourse starts in 6:26, and its special solemnity is marked by the four-fold use of the *"amen, amen"* (vv26,32,47,53), continually drawing attention to the significance of the points being made. As elsewhere in the gospel, the use of *amen* refers to the faithfulness of God and his promises. In John it is always used in the double form for emphasis, and no doubt alludes to the name of God as expressed in Isaiah 65:16 ("the God of *amen*"). The discourse begins with a reference to the mistaken motives which people had for coming to Jesus. This verse (v26) may well provide the clue for the right understanding of the whole chapter. John knows that Jesus does work miracles and perform signs and meet people's material needs, but to think of the signs merely on that level is to misunderstand them. Their object is to display the significance of Jesus. In the context of the eucharist, therefore, the words convey a warning not to think of the signs of Christian worship apart from their meaning, which is always to be found by reference to the person of Jesus on whom the Father has set his seal, and to the new life which is his free gift (v27). People are therefore to work not for material food, but they are "to work the work of God" (v28), which means that they are to continue to put their faith (*pisteuete*) in him whom God sent (vv28-29). Some manuscripts here have the aorist tense (*pisteusete*) which would imply that they are to come to faith in Jesus. The present tense, supported by the best manuscripts, fits the context better with the reference to the continual task of the Christian.

The response of Jesus elicits a further question: "What sign (*semeion*) are you doing that we may see and believe you (*pisteusomen soi*)" (v30). Here the aorist tense of *pisteuein* (believe) is rightly used, but in a different construction from the verb's use in the preceding verse. In verse 29 it means "continue to put your faith in Jesus", whereas in verse 30 the meaning is to "express our belief in what you say". The sign alludes to the eucharist which is the church's experience of Christ's act of salvation. So the discourse on manna introduces the contrast between the salvation effected under the Old Covenant, with reference not only to the experience of the Exodus but also to the rabbinic understanding of manna as signifying the Torah, as shown in the *Mekilta* (Lyonnet 1974:225). Borgen (1965:61-97,147-191) considers John 6:31-58 against the background of Jewish midrashic exegesis and concludes that John is arguing that the life-giving power of the Torah is now transferred to Jesus, who gives life not only to Israel but to the world. In doing this John uses not only the context of the Sinai covenant, but also the language used of Wisdom, especially in the combination of "coming", "eating" and "drinking" (Borgen 1965:154-155). If, as Borgen argues, verses 51 to 58 are an essential part of the Johannine midrash, the eucharistic allusions cannot be overlooked. But John's concern here, as elsewhere, is not with the eucharist as such, but rather with the person of Jesus. He is using eucharistic language to help his readers see not only that the Old Testament understanding of Torah and Wisdom finds fulfilment in Jesus, but also that the worship of the church, as expressed in the eucharist, has no meaning apart from its reference to Christ and his work.

Caird (1980:55) in commenting on verse 53 expresses a similar understanding – "the Eucharist is the source of John's language, not the theme or referent of the discourse". It is with reference to this chapter that Borgen (1965:190-191) describes Cullmann's approach (1953:93-102) as bringing "to the foreground that which really forms the background". Though Borgen recognizes the high regard which John has for the eucharist itself, he believes that in chapter 6 "ideas from traditions about manna and the well, and wisdom and halakhic principles of agency have been interwoven with the eucharistic phrases in a midrashic paraphrase". Such a view is confirmed by the position of chapter 6 between the theological discourses of chapters 5, 7 and 8 regarding the person and authority of Jesus. The eucharistic allusions help the readers or hearers of the gospel to see that in their worship they express their faith in the risen Lord and are united with him through the Spirit. "There is no conflict between Word and Sacrament in John 6, because both lead to the Incarnate One" (Borgen 1965:188). This remark of Borgen is the correct description of the relation between word and sacrament, and answers the objections of scholars who speak from a post-Reformation context. Moloney (1975) similarly argues both for the unity of the discourse in John 6 and for the congruence of faith and the sacrament.

Reference to the text of chapter 6 confirms this view. In answer to the claim of the Jews (v31) that "our fathers ate the manna in the wilderness, as scripture says 'He gave them bread from heaven to eat' ", Jesus, using the introductory formula *amen, amen,* makes two points. First, it was God, not Moses, who gave them bread from heaven. The reference to Moses helps to link this chapter with the discourses in chapters 5 and 7, showing once again that Jesus is fulfilling all that Moses said. This is perhaps the reason why the perfect tense *dedoken* (has given) used in verse 32a (according to the best mss), in contrast with the aorist (*edoken*, he gave) in the quotation in verse 31. The bread from heaven has a double meaning, referring both to the manna which came from the sky (Ex 16:13-15) and to the gift of the Torah which comes from God. The use of the perfect tense combined, as here, with the aorist (Louw 1967:29f) indicates that the gift is a continuing gift, not abrogated but fulfilled by the coming of Jesus. What God gave to Israel is still his gift, but the gift is Jesus Christ, the true bread from heaven.

So the second point made by Jesus' reply asserts that the gift of the true bread is being made now. The use of the present tense (*didosi*) indicates not only the historical act of the gift of Christ, but the continual giving of the Son to the Christian community as it meets to worship the risen Lord and enacts the *anamnesis* of his incarnation and self-giving in the eucharist. The tenses of the participles of the verbs need to be noted. Verse 33 uses the present tense – "The bread of God is he who *comes* down from heaven and *gives* life to the world", describing the ongoing act of Christ, which is not only an act of past history. Christians will recognize the allusions to the Lord who comes to meet them in their worship, witnessed by the use of *marana tha* (come, Lord) in eucharistic contexts (1 Cor 16:22; Rev 22:20; Did 10:6). Outsiders will see only ambiguity. The people's reply is a request to be given this bread (cf 4:15) at all times. The request is couched in similar terms to the petition of the Lord's Prayer (Mt 6:11), where *epiousios* (daily) may well refer to the gift of Christ himself, as Origen argues (*de Orat* 27) with a reference to John 6. Origen does not refer to the eucharistic bread in his long discussion, since, like John, he is concerned to stress the source of the true food in Jesus, though he knows well enough that the eucharist is the sign of the Lord's presence and self-giving (*Comm in ev Ioh* 32:24; Preuschen 1903:468). Just as Philo (*LegAll* 3:169-176) allegorizes manna and describes the word of God (*logos theou*) as food of the soul (Barrett 1978:288), so Jesus is here described as the true word of God, the true Torah (Suggit 1984:104-107). The statement of verse 35 – "I am (*ego eimi*) the bread of life" – completes the identification. He is to be acclaimed not as a figure of past history, but as the one who has come down (v38) from heaven, that is from God, and who continues to come to meet his people in their worship. The use of the perfect tense in verse 38 (to which attention is drawn by its repetition in v42) is a good example of what Louw believes to be the true semantic value of the perfect, stressing the content rather than the temporal aspect of the verb. His suggestion (1967:30) that the use of the perfect here gives added precision to the concept of coming down is exactly the meaning which John wishes to convey. No distinction can be made between the Jesus of history and the Christ of faith. In verse 41 the one who came down from heaven (*ho katabas*) is the same as the one who continues to come (cf Cullmann 1976:14).

In verse 35 – "He who comes to me will not hunger and he who believes in me will never thirst" – there may be an allusion to baptism or to eucharist, or to both. John is here referring to the centrality of Jesus in words which the Old Testament applies to Wisdom (e g Sir 24:19-21), and it matters little whether the reference is to baptism or eucharist, for in either case the really significant fact is the person of Jesus, the risen Lord, in whom men and women are called to put their faith.

Verses 35 to 50 certainly dispel any idea that John thought of baptism or eucharist as automatic means guaranteeing salvation. They show the fulfilment of Old Testament prophecies concerning the new covenant which God will make with his people (Is 54:13; Jer 31:31-34; Lyonnet 1974:222-223), which has been effected in the coming of Christ. The Jews are told clearly (v36) that though they have seen Jesus and his signs, they do not believe. Once again we see the necessary ambiguity of signs, whether the signs are the person of Jesus and what he has done or whether they are the sacraments of the church. Their meaning can be understood only by those who make their act of faith, which involves, among other things, the deliberate adoption of a particular basis for the interpretation of scripture and of the person of Christ. The presence of the outward sign does not necessarily lead to the understanding or acceptance of the thing signified, any more than the sight of Jesus in the flesh necessarily led to faith in him as one who had come from God. "No-one can come to me unless the Father who sent me draw him, and I will raise him up on the last day" (v44). Durkin (1987) reasonably suggests that this is part of a eucharistic hymn, the hymnic quality being marked by the repetition of the refrain "I will raise him up on the last day" (vv39,40,44,54), while the context can imply that the Father draws communicants to Christ as they receive the eucharistic elements. This accounts for the tension in John between realized and futurist eschatology, which "reaches a peak in this chapter" (Durkin 1987:168). Pierce (1960), commenting on the drama of the fourth gospel, thinks that for John

> there were no first and no last days, only today. Only the day he knew Jesus and received life through him. Life that was one long participle: the light was coming into the world.

This reference back to John 1:9 not only stresses the dramatic nature of the gospel, but also fits very well into the eucharistic context of chapter 6: the one who will come is the one who constantly comes in the eucharist, just as later on (vv51,58) the past too is brought into the present in the eucharist. The only other metaphorical use of the verb "to draw" in the fourth gospel occurs at 12:32, where it refers primarily to the exaltation of Christ on the cross, by which the drawing of believers to himself is made possible and which is proclaimed in the eucharist.

The stress on the action of God and the need of faith (v47) is a necessary prelude to what most scholars recognize as a section where the eucharistic allusions cannot be avoided. The section should be considered as starting at verse 47 and ending at verse 58. Verse 47, with the double *amen*, stresses faith as the prerequisite for eternal life (*zoe aionios*); verse 58 forms the *inclusio*, with the words "he will live for ever" (*zesei eis ton aiona*). Within this section verses 53 to 58, again introduced by *amen, amen,* display the real thrust of the whole passage. Verse 54 repeats the words of verse 47, but now the prerequisite for eternal life is described as "eating my flesh and drinking my blood". The language here can scarcely be interpreted without reference to the eucharist. It is true that John talks of the flesh (*sarx*) of Jesus, whereas the accounts of the institution of the eucharist in the gospels and in 1 Corinthians 11:24 refer to the body (*soma*) of Jesus, but Jeremias (1966:198-201) argues convincingly that the original Hebrew or Aramaic was *basar, bisra*, which would most naturally be translated by *sarx* in Greek, which was later changed to *soma* (body) especially for the sake of Gentiles. The Hebraic phrase "flesh and blood" refers to human beings, or human life, as is shown in the New Testament in Matthew 16:17.

For this reason Brooks (1963:297-298) believes that "to eat Jesus' flesh and drink his blood is none other than to accept his true humanity". He goes on to urge that John has used eucharistic language to present "the radical demand to accept the true humanity of the bringer of salvation", and in so doing "he has given the reader his understanding of the meaning of the eucharist – namely a reminder, or witness of the reality of the humanity of Jesus". This is a particularly interesting understanding in view of the not uncommon belief that John's christology took "the form of a naive docetism" (Käsemann 1968:26). Dunn (1971:336-337) with a view similar to that of Brooks, whom he quotes with approval, believes that the orthodox reaction to the challenge of docetism "led to a literalistic interpretation of the Lord's Supper and an over-emphasis on the physical act".

The strangeness of the language of John 6:53-56 certainly deserves special notice. Jews would find the concept of eating the flesh of Jesus difficult enough, but drinking his blood would seem to be quite impossible (Lev 17:10-14). The earliest formulation of the words of Jesus would seem to be represented in 1 Corinthians 11:25 – "This cup is the new covenant in my blood", where the identification of the wine with the blood of Jesus is not made. John's form of the words seems to represent a later understanding which emphasized the reality both of Jesus' death (and therefore of his humanity) and of his presence with the disciples in their eucharist.

It is certainly true that an early reaction to docetism was to stress the literal meaning of the words of institution, as is shown especially in Ignatius (*Rom* 7:3; *Smy* 7:1), but the constant stress in the fourth gospel is on the reality of the unity between God and human beings in Jesus, so that Dunn sees John as providing "the bridge between the earliest Wisdom christology of Paul and the subsequent Son christology of the classic creeds" (1980:214). Although it is true enough that John firmly fixes the locus of God's action in the historical Jesus, his understanding of the unity between Jesus and his disciples is closely related to his understanding of the unity between the Father and the Son (17:20-24). As Käsemann says (1968:68), "the unity of the community may not be detached from the unity of Father and Son which is its foundation".

The use of eucharistic language in John 6:47-58 is therefore to show that this unity between the disciples and God in and through Jesus Christ is demonstrated in the eucharist. To partake of the eucharist is to express one's faith in the reality of the revelation of God in the person of Jesus. Verse 50 refers to the bread which comes down (present tense) from heaven: verses 51 and 58 identify this bread which *comes down* from heaven with the bread which *came down* from heaven, the historical person of Jesus whose origin is from God (*ek tou theou* 8:42) or from heaven (*ek tou ouranou* 3:31). What is true of Jesus is equally true of those who believe in him (1:13; 17:16): the unity of the disciples with Jesus is expressed by eating the flesh and drinking the blood of the Son of Man, which cannot but refer to the eucharist. This however is not regarded as some automatic means of salvation but rather as the supreme occasion for encountering by faith the saving act of God in Christ.

Lohse (1961) represents the belief of many who hold that

although verses 51c to 58 cannot but refer to the eucharist, they are an ecclesiastical redaction, and not part of the "original gospel", whatever this description may mean. This opinion is influenced by a view of the sacraments which sees them as somehow contrasted with the proclamation of the word, as has been mentioned in chapter 1. If however the sacraments are seen primarily as a witness to the Lordship of the risen Christ present among his people, there is no contrast between their function and that of the preached word. Both are means of grace, since both help people to believe in the Lordship of the Word made flesh. So as John talks of Jesus and his feeding of the multitude he uses language which helps his hearers or readers to understand the significance of their liturgical acts. Goppelt (1982:302) has a realistically balanced view:

> John combined here in an impressive way word and sacrament. From Jn 6:51c on, the sacrament did not simply take its place alongside the word. Rather the word became, as it were, concentrated in the direction of the sacrament, and the sacrament received in this way verbal character. What was declared here as necessary for salvation was not an ecclesiastical institution, but the word that had become flesh.

Such a view of this passage is confirmed by the following verses (vv 60-71). John's gospel is in the form of a biography, or at least it takes the reader back to a time contemporary with Jesus. John cannot therefore have Jesus talk of baptism and eucharist in an anachronistic way, but the language which he uses is such as to alert the later Christian disciple to realize that the Lord Jesus is as present in the eucharist as he was with Peter and James and John and the rest.

In John's account the realism of Jesus' words offended many of the disciples because he was claiming for himself the prerogative of God alone – the ability to give life (vv47,58). But for later disciples a similar problem arose with the eucharist, a problem which has been specially prominent since the Reformation. John therefore makes it clear (v62) that the meaning both of the incarnation and of the eucharist can be understood only after the resurrection and the return of the incarnate Word to the glory of the Father (17:5). The meaning of the eucharist, like the meaning of the person of Christ, is to be found in the unity between Father and Son. Verse 63 is often regarded as crucial to the understanding of the whole passage: "It is the Spirit who gives life; and the flesh (*sarx* is of no avail; the words which I have spoken to you are Spirit and life". The Spirit presumably refers to the Holy Spirit, the giver of life, as is indicated in 7:37-38 and 4:14. But the Spirit is here identified with the words of Jesus: rightly so, because the Spirit's function is always to bear witness to the relevance and significance of the life, death and resurrection of Jesus and of his teaching (14:26; cf Hanson 1960:75-77). This is also the purpose of the sacraments, but without the action of the Spirit enabling the disciples to put their faith in Jesus and his words, the sacraments are in danger of becoming flesh without spirit, signs without meaning. So the words of Jesus, like the words of Torah, (*Mekilta* on Ex 15:26, quoted by Barrett 1978:305) are life-giving, but only, as verse 64 makes clear, for those who have faith (cf 1:12).

The conclusion of the whole pericope of chapter 6 issues in the confession of Peter – "You have words of eternal life, and we have believed and we know that you are the Holy One of God" (vv69-70) – and in the prediction of the treachery of Judas, one of the chosen twelve. Here is the contrast between those who recognize Jesus as the sign of life, and those who see only his outward appearance and judge him accordingly (7:24). "We have believed (*hemeis pepisteukamen*) and have come to know that you are the Holy One of God" (v69). The perfect tense draws attention to the past act of confession which results in the new status of believers, while the use of the pronoun emphasises the difference between believers and non-believers. This contrast of views persisted at the time when John wrote for later disciples, who could find the meaning of baptism and eucharist only by their expression of faith in him to whom these rites bore witness.

5

Jesus, the giver of sight and life: John 9 & 11

The people here do things their own way. They are fighting to hold on to something and they know they have to act quickly before the heat in them dies down. It doesn't matter what happens afterwards. Because they want to feel everything still holds together in one piece. They want to believe there's a meaning in life and a reason for everything. Once that breaks there is no meaning, no reason, nothing: and that's too terrifying to think of. (Saul)

J Cope *The Rainmaker* (Heinemann 1971) 213

The light of the world

The call to Nathanael "Come and see" (Jn 1:46) is the call addressed to every reader of the gospel. As with the injunction of Jesus as reported in Mark "He who has ears to hear, let him hear" (e g Mk 4:9), so throughout the fourth gospel the meaning of the person of Jesus is carefully explained for those whose eyes and ears have been opened, and who are ready to use all their faculties to grow to a deeper understanding of God's action in Jesus and in themselves. The opening of the eyes and ears is effected by Jesus and not as a result of human effort. It is not

therefore surprising that the story of the healing of the deaf mute
(Mk 7:31-37) had from early times a prominent place in the
baptismal liturgy (Ambrose *Sacr* 1:1:2), indicating the need for
the candidate's ears to be opened by the Lord so as to be able
to hear the gospel. John writes in a similar way as he describes
the healing of blindness and the recovery of sight as due to the
action of Jesus.

The connection between the healing of blindness and Christian
baptism was made very early on. The opening words of Tertullian's *De Baptismo* refer to "the sacred sign (*sacramentum*) of
our water by which we are set free for eternal life by the washing
away of the sins of our original blindness (*pristinae caecitatis*)",
and the regular description from early times of the baptized as
illuminati (Lat) or *photisthentes* (Gk) is probably already to be
noted in the New Testament, as has been mentioned earlier. In
the fourth gospel especially the source of the light is described
as Jesus himself, the light of the world (Jn 1:9; 8:12). It may be,
as Godet suggested (1885:II,362), that the use of spittle to effect
healing in the account of the blind man in chapter 9 was meant
to be "a symbol calculated to make the sufferers feel ... that their
cure emanated from *His Person Itself*" (italics original). It is
from the touch of Jesus and union with him that sight is given.

The account in chapter 9 concerns a man (*anthropos*, v1). The
suggestion that this deliberately refers to Adam may not be
overlooked. Certainly this is how Augustine understood it –
"This blind man is the human race", blind from birth because
of Adam's sin (*Tract in ev Ioh* 44:1, *PL* 34:1713; cf 34:9, *PL*
34:1655). *Anthropos* is frequently used in the Septuagint (e g
Gen 2:15) to translate the Hebrew *adam*. If this is John's
intention here, he is not really concerned to discuss the meaning
of original sin, other than to describe the human condition in its
alienation from God as a life without sight and meaning. Yet
there was a purpose in the man's blindness: "Neither did this
man sin nor did his parents, but he is in this state in order that
the works of God might be made manifest in him" (v3). It is as
though the original creation of Adam cannot be properly considered without reference to the redemption effected by Christ.
The incarnation of the Word of God, with the consequence of
the cross, was not something which God determined when his

first plan had failed through Adam's misuse of his free-will. Rather it was built into God's purposes from the start as the way in which God graciously gave human beings some sort of share in the freedom which belongs in its fullness to God alone, while at the same time he took steps to overcome the misuse which people seemed bound to make of this gracious gift.

The same idea finds expression in the letter to the Ephesians, which shows many similarities of thought and expression to the fourth gospel. In the apparently baptismal passage (Coutts 1957) of Ephesians 1:3-14 Christians are described as those who have been chosen in Christ before the foundation of the world to be God's holy people (v4). God's purpose from all time was to sum up the universe in Christ so that he might be seen to give meaning to the whole of God's creation (v10). So in John 9 the blind man is the symbol of human beings alienated from God who can be restored to their true nature and being only through the action of the incarnate Word (*logos*) of God, who embodies in his own person God's plan (*logos*) for his creation.

The carrying out of this plan is entrusted to the church, God's people, though it is entirely dependent on God's action in Christ. This explains the use of the pronouns in verse 4 – "*We* must carry out the works of him who sent *me*". Copyists were puzzled by the change of number and so made different attempts at harmonization. Dodd (1963:186) may be right in holding that this saying derives from a proverbial expression, but John uses it to describe the way in which the disciples are so united with Christ that their work can be described as his work. The wording recalls words uttered by Jesus on another sabbath – "My father is working until now, and I am working" (5:17). The work of God, effected in Jesus, is continued by him in his church. The same pattern recurs in John 20:21, where the mission of the Son is continued in and through the disciples. The work must be done in the light of the day, for the day is the sign of God's presence, the night the sign of his absence (Rev 21:25). So the meaning of verse 5 – "As long as I am in the world I am the light of the world" – is elucidated by verse 4. The presence of the Lord in the world is not restricted to the period of Jesus' incarnate life. "The day of Christ's presence", said Augustine, (*Tract in ev Ioh* 44:6; *PL* 34:1716) "is extended to the close of the age." His presence is carried on in his disciples (17:18-26; 20:21), who need to be continually aware of his light and to respond to it, else the light will be extinguished and the world will be left in darkness. The fourth gospel challenges believers to be bearers of the light of Christ. "Christianity exists", writes Küng (1978:126), "only where the memory of Jesus Christ is activated in theory and practice." John is saying the same thing but in different words: those who believe in the name of Christ will be children of light (8:12; 12:36), not only "having the light" and living in the light, but also revealing it to others. The Torah, which was the light for Israel (Ps 119:105), has now been replaced by the person of Christ. The argument which runs through 8:12-59 is now demonstrated in the sign of chapter 9.

The act of making clay with spittle was an act of creation, modelled on God's act of creation in Genesis 2:7 (Lindars 1972:343). By this act the man is restored to his true being. The very fact that this takes place on the sabbath, in direct contradiction to the Torah (Barrett 1978:358), is an indication of the continuation of God's work of creation by Jesus. The making of the clay and smearing it on the man's eyes is symbolic of the new creation. Just as Adam was formed from "dust from the earth" (Heb *'apar min-ha'adamah*; Gk, *choun apo tes ges*; Gen 2:7), so human beings are remade by the act of Christ. Admittedly *pelos* (clay) is used by John instead of the Septuagint *chous* (dust), but *pelos* is found in the well-known simile of the potter in Jeremiah 18:6, where the verb *yasar* (to form, make) is used in the Hebrew text as in Genesis 2:7. The connection of clay (*pelos*) with the creation narrative of Genesis seems to be assured by the use which Paul makes of the simile in Romans 9:19-24.

The clay is smeared on the man's eyes because the whole incident is in the context of Jesus as the bringer of light. In order to be recreated people have to have their eyes opened to see the meaning of life and to find it in Jesus. The word used in John 9:6 (*epechrisen*) really means "anointed". A few manuscripts (including B) read *epetheken* (placed on), which probably represents an assimilation to verse 15. *Epechrisen* is used again in verse 11 where there is no variant reading. Although the word has been used in Greek with the meaning "to anoint", "to smear", since the time of Homer, and although a "very striking parallel" in an inscription of 138 AD is quoted by Moulton and Milligan (1914-1929:251), the verb does not occur elsewhere in the New Testament. The New Testament writers were well aware of the relation between the verb *chriein* (anoint) and the title *Christos* ("the anointed one", see 2 Cor 1:21; Lk 4:18; Ac 4:27; 10:38; Heb 1:9; cf too 1 Jn 2:20,27). It is therefore likely that John deliberately used this word instead of *epetheken* which the grammatical construction of verse 6 would strictly require, though it should be noted that the inscription already mentioned uses *epichriein* in the same construction as is found in John. Certainly the man in the narrative knew what had happened to him, since verse 11 represents him as saying that Jesus anointed (*epechrisen*) his eyes. In so far as baptism was regarded as the way by which a person became a Christian (in Christ, the anointed one) the use of the word in this context indicates a baptismal allusion. Augustine certainly understood it as such (*Tract in ev Ioh* 44:2; *PL* 34:1714), but his interpretation shows the danger of assuming that contemporary baptismal practice may be read back into the New Testament. For Augustine the anointing with clay symbolized the making of a catechumen, while the washing in Siloam symbolized baptism. Although there was presumably some kind of teaching given even in New Testament times before a candidate was baptized (1 Cor 11:2; 15:1-3; 2 Th 2:15; 3:6; 1 Tim 6:20; 2 Tim 1:14; cf Lk 1:4), there is no evidence that there was any preliminary rite prior to baptism.

The baptismal allusion is continued and made more explicit by the command to go and wash in the pool of Siloam. The use of *kolumbethra* for pool has already been noted in the comments made earlier on John 5:2, where the view was expressed that any reference to baptism was in the background. The situation in chapter 9 is very different, as Brown has noted (1965:64-66). Not only does the command to wash recall baptismal imagery, but the name of the pool, *Siloam*, is carefully explained as meaning "he who has been sent" (v7). It is worth noting that although the description of Jesus as the one whom the Father sent is frequent in John, it is especially common in chapters 7 and 8 (7:16,18, 28,29,33; 8:16,18,26,29,42) and is found again at 9:4. The interpretation of *Siloam* as "he who has been sent" (*apestalmenos*) is quite clearly intended to draw attention to Jesus, so that "to wash in (*eis*) the pool of Siloam" would be equivalent to being washed, or baptized, into (*eis*) Christ (e g Gal 3:27). The fact that John usually favours *pempein* as the verb meaning "to send" does not discount this conclusion, since John regularly uses synonyms interchangeably as a stylistic device, of which a particularly good example is furnished by 21:15-17. John 20:21 clearly shows that *apostellein* is no different in meaning from *pempein*: "As the Father has sent (*apestalken*) me, so am I sending (*pempo*) you."

The rest of the narrative of chapter 9 continues with baptismal allusions: the start of a new life, entailing a break with the past, is marked by the confession of Jesus as the Christ (v22). The healed man, not his parents, has to explain what has happened and who has opened his eyes (v21). His rejoinder to the Pharisees – "Do you too want to become his disciples" – implies that through the granting of sight to him by Jesus he has himself become a disciple. Verse 34 contrasts the Pharisees, who are expert in Torah, with the man who was "altogether born in sins", who through his restored sight and new life now presumes to teach them. The account proceeds with Jesus' question "Do you believe on the Son of Man?" (v36). The meaning of baptism always demands the expression of faith: hence the importance of the aorist subjunctive. Once his question had been answered, the man expressed his belief and worshipped Jesus (v38). The new dispensation brought by Jesus is paradoxically expressed in verse 39 along the lines of Isaiah 6:9-10, a text quoted in John 12:40 and widely used, no doubt especially to explain the reason for the unbelief of most Jews. It leads on to the next question and answer (vv40-41) which reinforce the baptismal allusions. To the question "Are we also blind?" Jesus replies "If you were blind you would not have any sin; but as in fact you say 'we see', your sin remains". There can be no forgiveness without the recognition of sin and repentance. This entails turning to Christ and receiving new sight. Any doubt about the symbolic nature of the healing miracle is dispelled by these two verses.

The relation of John 9 to John 8

Painter (1979) in a study of John's use of symbolism took chapter 9 as a case-study. He rightly saw that the emphasis in the fourth gospel is christocentric rather than sacramental. There is no doubt that here as elsewhere John is concerned with the centrality of Jesus and his work. This can be seen especially by considering the context of chapter 9. The two previous chapters (7 and 8) were especially concerned with the person of Jesus, and 7:40-52 describes the various opinions which were held about him. The passage concludes with the Pharisees' response to Nicodemus' plea for a fair hearing to be accorded to Jesus – "search the scriptures and see that a (or, perhaps, the) prophet does not arise from Galilee". Since 7:53-8:11 is admitted on all sides to have formed no part of the original fourth gospel, the next verse (8:12) begins a long section on the person of Jesus, starting with his claim "I am the light of the world". Verses 21 to 24 contrast the position of the Pharisees with that of Jesus. They will die in their sins unless they make their act of faith (aorist – *pisteusete*) that "I am he" (*ego eimi*), where the allusion to Isaiah 43:10 should not be overlooked (Barrett 1978:341-342). Isaiah 43:10 in the Septuagint reads:

> You were my witnesses ... says the Lord God, and the servant whom I chose, that you may know and believe (*pisteusete*) and understand that I am he (*ego eimi*). Before me there was no other god, and there will not be another after me.

Isaiah both here and elsewhere (42:8; 48:12) seems to refer to Exodus 3:14 and Augustine (*Tract in ev Ioh* 39:8; *PL* 34:1679) has no doubt that John intends this reference, drawing the conclusion that Jesus is claiming to be God. Dodd (1954:94) gives reasons for holding that the Hebrew phrase rendered by the Greek *ego eimi* (Heb *'ani hu'*) was considered to be the name of God. This therefore would mean that the name given to YHWH in the Old Testament is now to be ascribed to Jesus. Belief in Jesus as revealing the nature of God is thus (according to Jn 8:24) the condition for finding life and forgiveness of sins. The same idea is expressed in Philippians 2:9, where "the name above every name" would seem to mean that the exalted Jesus is accorded a status equal to that of YHWH, whose unutterable name is superior to any other name.

Those who fail to recognize the revelation of God in Jesus will die in their sins, a phrase repeated from 8:21, where it is dangerous to try to find a difference between the singular (sin) of that verse and the plural in 8:24, in view of the New Testament idiom, following Aramaic and Hebrew, of using the distributive singular for the plural (Blass and Debrunner 1961:77). When therefore the healed blind man is told by the Pharisees "*You* were born entirely in sins, and do *you* teach us?" (9:34) we are given a fine example of Johannine irony. The one who has recognized that Jesus is from God (9:33) and believes in him (9:38) is the one who will not die in his sin, since he has found forgiveness and new life, while those who think they see and yet do not recognize Jesus are blind. Their sin remains (9:41). Chapter 8 continues with further reference to the person of Jesus. The Jews are told "when you exalt the Son of Man, then you will know that I am he (*ego eimi*)" (v28), where the reference is to the exaltation on the cross, which is also Christ's exaltation in glory (12:32-34). The condition of being a disciple of Christ is to abide in his word, whereby a person finds the truth which leads to freedom. This leads on to a further dialogue concerning the person of Jesus who is represented as the son of his Father, God (v42), whereas the Pharisees have the devil for their father (v44), in spite of their claim to be children of Abraham (vv39,53). The dialogue culminates in the pronouncement of verse 58 – "Before Abraham was, I am (*ego eimi*)". This theme of the person of Jesus is resumed in chapter 10, leading up to the claim in 10:30 "I and the Father are one (*hen* – a unity)".

Jesus as Lord then and now

There is therefore little doubt that John is primarily concerned to describe the person of Jesus. As the giver of sight he gives new meaning to the life of human beings who without him are alienated from God (cf Eph 2:12-13). John however is concerned not only with the Jesus of history, but with the risen Lord present in the community for whom he writes. The Lord's presence with his people is declared especially in baptism and eucharist. It is in these acts of worship that the work of Jesus is proclaimed and represented so that they become ways not only in which the action of God's love in Christ is symbolically re-enacted, but also of enabling the participants to share in Christ's death and resurrection and the new life which results from it. Baptism marks the beginning of this new life, for it involves the recognition of Jesus as the one who reveals the nature of God.

Although therefore one can accept Painter's view (1979:31) that the symbolism of John is primarily intended to lead people to faith in Jesus, and though it may be true enough that John wishes to correct misunderstandings of baptism and eucharist, the language of John is such as to lead his readers to consider their own position and the meaning of that ritual act by which they became members of the new community of Christ. They had found meaning for their life through their faith in Jesus which they would have solemnly expressed at their baptism. It is this which distinguishes them from the unbelieving Jews (8:30-31). They might well have considered their own baptism as the time when scales fell from their eyes, similar to the experience of Paul as described in Acts 9:18. This does not mean that John thought of baptism (or eucharist) as some kind of mechanical rite by which forgiveness and sight are assured for all time, nor that he was primarily concerned with the cultic acts in themselves. Rather John used language which alluded to these acts of worship in order to show his readers or hearers the real meaning of their expression of faith in Christ and to confirm them in their faith.

Baptism, like the restoration of the blind man's sight, is due to an act of God: but its significance and value is appreciated only by those who have put their faith in Christ and who persevere as his disciples. It is true, as Painter says (1979:31), that "John's use of symbols is more inclusive than the sacraments ... and ... he attributes no exclusive function to these rites". Nevertheless by writing the way he does, he is continually reminding his readers that their cultic acts are not empty signs but expressions of God's redemptive love in Christ and occasions for the expression or confirmation of their faith in, and union with, him.

This view is strengthened by seeing chapter 9 in the context of the whole section 8:12 to 12:50, which begins with Jesus' claim "I am the light of the world". It ends with the summary of Christ's work (12:44-50), in which themes of the whole section are resumed. 12:46, with its reference back to 8:12, expresses the meaning of the incarnation and of the sign of chapter 9: "I have come as light into the world so that everyone who believes in me may avoid remaining in darkness." He comes as light so as to save the world (12:47): those who refuse to accept the light will be judged by "the word which I spoke" which is in fact the word of the Father. This division between believers and non-believers is a theme which has been prominent throughout the whole section. In 8:21-23 the distinction between those "from below" and those "from above" is seen as permanent, and in the subsequent discourse Jesus who has come from God is contrasted with the Pharisees whose father is the devil (8:42-44), and the final verse of chapter 8 (v59) describes the hostility of the unbelievers – "Thy took up stones to stone him".

Chapter 9 describes what happened when a man received his sight from Jesus and believed in him. There was a division between those who were prepared to accept the sign as a credential of Jesus' person and those who refused to do so (9:16). The healed man was himself forced to take sides and declare himself. As a result he was expelled from the synagogue (vv22,34), in the sense that he was no longer considered to be a member of God's people. What happened to him was to be the lot of all who believed in Jesus (16:2). Henceforth they would have to join the new community united with Jesus (15:1-7; 17:11-26). This is what faith in Jesus as the Christ involves, and this is the meaning of baptism.

The nature of the new community and its relation to Jesus is described in 10:10-18, where the words of Jesus once again cause a division (v19). The formation of the new community is now closely linked to the death and resurrection of Jesus (vv15-18). This leads on to a fuller explication of the person of Jesus, resulting once again in the hostility of the unbelieving Jews (v39). As though to keep the baptismal implications before the readers' eyes the chapter concludes with references to John the Baptist and his baptism, in which he is contrasted with Jesus and the signs which he performed.

Jesus the giver of life: John 11

The account of the raising of Lazarus which follows in chapter 11 prefigures the Passion Narrative. Morton Smith's belief (1982) that the story arose from certain initiation practices of Jesus in which a death and resurrection was simulated after the fashion of the mystery rites, has little to commend it. But there is much in the narrative as John relates it which reflects the experience of the early Christian community. Lazarus can be seen as the type of Christian disciples, and what happened to him is the experience of every Christian. Like Lazarus (11:36) the disciples are loved by the Lord, being regularly addressed in the epistles as beloved (*agapetoi*, e g 1 Jn 4:1). Like him, they have been called by name (11:43) from death into life. Like him, as sheep of the good shepherd Jesus, they listen to, and obey, his voice (10:3-5). Like him (11:44) they are handed over to the care of the Christian community when they have found life in Christ. The parallelism is continued further: as disciples who have experienced the new life in Christ through baptism are privileged to share with him and other Christians in the Lord's Supper, so Lazarus is found at supper with Jesus and the disciples (12:2). As every Christian is called to be a witness to Jesus (15:27), so Lazarus is threatened with death by the high-priests because his new life is a standing testimony to Jesus, and crowds come to see him (12:9-11).

It is not difficult therefore to consider chapter 11 as reflecting the experience of every Christian who has been raised to life by Christ. Morton Smith (1982:14-17) claims to have discovered a fragment of a letter of Clement of Alexandria in which Clement said that when Mark came to Alexandria with his gospel "he composed a more spiritual gospel for those who were being perfected". Regrettably this fragment has apparently been lost, but it appears to refer to the story of Lazarus and to interpret it with reference to baptism. If this is so, then, as Brown remarks (1974:485), we have important early evidence for such an interpretation.

There are other indications that John intended chapter 11, like chapter 9, to remind readers of the gospel of their own experience of the start of their life as Christians. Whatever the origin of the Lazarus story may have been, in its final form John is careful to link its interpretation to chapter 9, as Lindars (1972:379) points out. Lazarus' death, like the man's blindness (9:3) is for the glory of God (11:4). The need to walk in the daylight (11:9) is paralleled by 9:4-5, and indeed the reference in 11:9 to the light of the world serves to connect this with the claim of Jesus in 8:12, by which he can give sight to the blind. Any doubt that the giving of life and the giving of sight are intimately connected should be dispelled by the deliberate reference in 11:37 to the healing of the blind man. The light which the blind man is given leads to new life, in pursuance of Jesus' promise "He who follows me ... will have the light of life" (8:12), a statement which Augustine (*Tract in ev Ioh* 34:5, *PL* 34:1654) refers back to Psalm 36:9 "With you is the fountain of life, and in your light we shall see light". Like YHWH, Jesus is shown not only as the giver of light, but as the light itself, and the giver of life.

Once again, however, the account of the raising of Lazarus is not primarily concerned with baptism, nor is it simply concerned with the story of the raising of a dead man to life. John has narrated the story, which presumably he accepted as a historical event, in a way which symbolically describes the person and work of Jesus. In this respect the climax is reached in the claim of verses 25 and 26 – "I am resurrection and I am life. He who believes in me shall live even if he dies, and no-one who is alive who believes in me will ever die". The gift of life which Jesus gives is therefore not simply physical life, nor is it a mere continuation of our mortal life. Life becomes a symbol, standing for life in its fullness and of a new quality, what existentialists might well call "authentic being".

The claim of Jesus in the fourth gospel is that true life can be found only by abiding in Christ, since he is the life. This was the claim accepted by Paul – "For me life is Christ" (*to zen Christos* – Phil 1:21). This life is received by faith, when a person in obedience to God's word becomes a Christian through baptism. But life in this sense also involves death, for the new relationship

effected in baptism between God and human beings is due to
the death of Jesus on the cross. The account of Lazarus therefore "is also the story of Jesus going to face death in order to
conquer death" (Dodd 1954:367). As such it forms a fitting
prelude to the Passion Narrative. But the story is told to show
too that to find life disciples must share in the death of Jesus.
So it is that Thomas says to his fellow-disciples "Let us too go
with him that we may die with him" (11:16). The name Thomas
is pointedly translated into Greek, Didymus, the twin, to remind
Christian readers that Thomas is their twin, their *Doppelgänger*.

So although the narrative of the raising of Lazarus is concerned
with the person and work of Christ it contains an abundance of
allusions to the way in which Christian disciples through baptism have died to their old selves and have found the meaning of
life, life in its fullest sense, in their union with Christ. The story
of Lazarus, connected as it is with the story of the recovery of
the blind man's sight in chapter 9, shows that the gift of sight,
the gift of finding the meaning of life in Jesus, is intimately
connected with the gift of life itself. As such the two narratives
describe the gracious gifts of God to believers, and draw attention to the implications which their acceptance entails. The
fuller meaning of these is expounded in the following chapters
of the gospel.

6

Liturgy and life I:
The night before the passion

Well now; there's nothing in nor out o' the world
Good except truth: yet this, the something else,
What's this then, which proves good yet seems untrue?
This that I mixed with truth, motions of mine
That quickened, made the inertness malleolable
O' the gold was not mine, – what's your name for this?
Are means to the end, themselves in part the end?
Is fiction, which makes fact alive, fact too?
The somehow may be thishow.

R Browning *The Ring and the Book* I:698-706

The mystery of the incarnation and of the eucharist: John 13:1-30

Chapter 13 introduces a new phase in the gospel. From now on the emphasis changes. Instead of a ministry and addresses directed to the crowd or to the Jews, Jesus is now concerned with his disciples. John therefore describes the conditions of discipleship and the way in which disciples are united with their Lord, sharing in his life, his passion and his glory. But in order to do that effectively he needs to describe the significance of the ministry of Jesus, which he does with remarkable vividness in his account of the foot-washing in chapter 13, the context of which is the Last Supper. The whole section 13:1-30 can rightly be called the mystery of the incarnation and of the eucharist.

The word "mystery" has been deliberately chosen for its New Testament sense of God's secret purpose declared in Christ (see above p 16). It is in a similar sense that the sacraments have been called from early times "the holy mysteries" (*ta hagia musteria*) since in them is set forth and made present the purpose of God for his creation effected in Christ. John 13 brings together the theme of the incarnation and that of the sacraments, and the importance of the chapter is marked by its position in the gospel, as it introduces the new stage of the narrative. Most editions of the New Testament, both Greek and in translation, indicate this by having a significant gap before 13:1. We may not deny the connection of chapter 13 with the preceding chapters, but the structure and contents of this chapter seem to indicate that the evangelist is here drawing out the meaning of all that has been previously related. If it is true that every episode of John contains the main themes of the gospel as a whole (cf Dodd 1954:384), this is especially true of 13:1-30. With this chapter we are entering upon the narration of the most solemn and momentous phase of the gospel. The pericope therefore forms a very fitting introduction to a consideration of the theme of the gospel and the worship of the church.

The opening verse (13:1) sets the scene: the use of the particle *de*, as often in the fourth gospel (Abbott 1906:104), introduces a new incident. For not only does *de* mark the introduction of a new fact (e g 3:1,23; 4:6), but it is also used to introduce a new incident or narrative of real significance (e g 6:16; 11:1). It is as though the evangelist is inviting the reader to consider this additional fact in the light of all that has gone before. The RSV rightly translates *de* as "now".

The sentence as a whole is also carefully and solemnly structured with a series of participles and with phrases of deep theological content. The opening phrase "before the feast of the Passover" serves to do two things: it sets what follows in the context of the Passover and contrasts this Passover with "the Passover of the Jews" (2:13; 6:4; 11:55). The true Passover is Jesus himself. This is the view not only of John who describes the death of Jesus as occurring at the time when the Paschal lamb was slain, but it is also upheld explicitly by Paul (1 Cor 5:7). In this way John, as is well known, is careful not to describe the Last Supper as a Passover meal (compare the irony of 18:28). 13:1 therefore resembles 12:1, where the anointing is similarly set in a Paschal context and also needs to be understood against the background of the cross. In both cases the implication is that now in Jesus the true meaning of "the Passover of the Jews" has been declared. As a result the Passover which the Jews continue to celebrate is different from the Christian *Pascha* which has taken its place.

The note of time is followed immediately by words which make it clear that Jesus knew all that was to happen. The participle "knowing" (*eidos*) of verse 1 is taken up again in amplification in verse 3. Jesus' knowledge, however, is further stressed throughout the pericope. In verses 11 and 18 Jesus shows his awareness of Judas' intentions, and verse 7 assures Peter that he too will have knowledge later. So the act of foot-washing is firmly set in the context of Jesus' knowledge of his destiny and mission. Though the RSV translates *eidos* by "when Jesus knew ..." it is preferable to take it as circumstantial or descriptive, "knowing as he did ...": it describes his whole attitude to his task, as John represents it. Jesus has always known who he is and from where he has come. In 18:37 his knowledge of his origin and purpose is adduced as the grounds for accepting the truth of his witness. The first verse of chapter 13 reminds the reader in solemn style of Jesus' knowledge, and the event which the chapter describes demonstrates the purpose of Jesus' coming. It is the cross which gives meaning to the whole work of Christ, from the conception to the ascension. Although Bultmann (1955b:53-55) notes the close connection between the cross and the whole of Jesus' life, as John represents it, he refuses to assign to the cross the importance which Schnackenburg (1968:158) rightly finds in the fourth gospel.

The hour had now come (13:1): anticipated from 2:4 the hour is the hour of the exaltation of the Son of Man, on the cross and in glory. In the previous chapter (12:23) it is made quite clear that the exaltation on the cross is the exaltation in glory. The hour of glory is also the hour of his return to the Father, to share in "the glory which I had with you before the world was" (17:5). But the glory of the return is preceded by reference to Christ's work in the world, again expressed in a participial phrase. The aorist *agapesas* (having loved) considers the work of Christ as a completed whole, and this is reinforced by the final four words which form the main clause of the verse – "he loved them to the end" (*eis telos*). This is the only use of *telos* in John, and John no doubt intends it to have more than a single meaning. The phrase can mean both "to the end" and "to the uttermost"; it can refer, in other words, to the temporal or the qualitative aspect of Jesus' love. The use of the corresponding verb (*telein*) occurs in John only in 19:28,30, and it would seem likely that in the latter case the cry of Jesus "it is accomplished" (*tetelestai*) is closely linked to the use of the phrase *eis telos* in 13:1, which is therefore full of meaning.

Jesus' love is for his own (*hoi idioi*). His own are those whom he has chosen (15:16) and who have responded in faith (10:3). In this way the disciples are distinguished from "his own" of 1:11, who are the Jews and who, so the gospel declares, rejected Jesus. The demonstration of Jesus' love is for those who are his. This is not a contradiction of 4:42 where Jesus is hailed as the saviour of the world. The purpose of Jesus' coming is to call all people into the new relationship with himself through which they may find life of the new age (3:16). His own are those who have responded in faith.

The first verse (13:1) therefore summarizes the meaning of 13:1-30. Set in the context of the Passover and the approaching cross the verse describes the mission and work of Christ and his union with his disciples. The same solemn style of narrative continues in the next sentence which begins in verse 2, though the two co-ordinate main clauses are not found until verse 4. They are introduced by two more participial phrases which define the circumstances more sharply. The first, "while supper was going on" (*deipnou ginomenou*), defines the occasion. There is good manuscript authority for reading the aorist *genomenou*. If the aorist is read, then the context would seem to demand that it be regarded as an ingressive aorist with the meaning "when supper had started". It seems clear enough that the supper was still continuing after the foot-washing (13:26).

"During supper" is therefore a good translation of either reading. If the present is read, and if it could be assumed that John was thinking of a similar procedure to that described in 1 Corinthians 11:24-25, then the foot-washing is described with particular vividness as occurring between the giving of the bread and the giving of the cup. Here is a clear indication that the act of foot-washing is meant to describe the meaning of the supper. Although *deipnon* can be used to describe any kind of supper (usually the main, evening meal) it is used by Paul (1 Cor 11:20) to refer to the eucharist, the Lord's supper, and in Revelation 19:9,17 it refers to the eschatological banquet of which the eucharist is an anticipation. It is frequently used in pagan sources to refer to a cultic meal.

What does *deipnon* mean in John? It is used only four times – 13:2,4; 21:20 (where it refers back to c 13) and 12:2. It would be incredible if John did not know the tradition preserved in the synoptics as well as by Paul that Jesus celebrated a supper with his disciples on the night before he died and that this was taken as the authority for the celebration of the church's eucharist. Since John dates the crucifixion to Nisan 14 the supper which he describes cannot be the Passover. Whether John is historically correct or not does not affect the interpretation of this chapter, for in any case the Passover forms the background of the incident. In view of the evidence of the synoptics and of Paul it would seem very reasonable to hold that John knew of the connection between this supper and the Christian eucharist and that he therefore had good reasons for not actually describing the institution of the eucharist.

In similar vein, Thüsing (1970:173), commenting on 19:34, ascribes the lack of an institution narrative to the evangelist's desire to affirm that the Spirit and the sacraments proceed from the death of Jesus. So John did not wish to complicate or destroy the force and clarity of this theological purpose. 6:51-58 shows that John does not deny, but knows and recognizes, the historical fact of the institution. He wanted rather, says Thüsing, to affirm it more impressively than could be done by repeating the synoptic account.

This whole chapter indeed is a good example of the thesis

upheld by Wright (1988:10) that "the indirect mode of reference employed in literature constitutes some of the most effective theology". The context is sufficiently clear to enable those who heard the narrative to see its relevance to their understanding of the eucharist. John had no need to describe what Christians regularly practised, just as he had no need to be like Matthew and Luke in recording the words of the Lord's Prayer. He is much more concerned with describing the meaning which lies behind the liturgical practices of the church. He is, as Smalley (1978:130) puts it, not really interested in the sacraments as such. But he is deeply concerned with the meaning which the sacraments set forth. Such a view brings to chapter 13 a unity which some commentators believe to be difficult to find, since there appear to be two themes imperfectly reconciled in a single narrative (cf Boismard 1964).

Deipnou ginomenou (during supper) therefore in 13:2, especially as it follows the reference to the Passover, sets the scene in such a way that the reader cannot but see the allusions to the eucharist. The second participial phrase in the same verse reinforces this understanding. It does not matter for our purpose how this phrase should be translated. What is clear is that (a) the act of foot-washing is carried out in the context of the supper and (b) at a time when one of the twelve has become the agent for the betrayal of Jesus. This is John's way of helping the reader or hearer of the gospel to consider whether he too may not be a traitor. Mere participation in the Lord's Supper is not enough. The synoptics achieve the same purpose in different ways (Mk 14:19f; Mt 26:22f; Lk 22:23): the presence of Judas at the Last Supper is the continual reminder of the possibility that the disciple of the Lord, united with his Lord in the eucharist, might nevertheless betray him. The mention of Judas and his intentions at this point confirms the belief that John is describing the supper where the eucharist was instituted.

The narrative (13:3) continues with another participial phrase – "Jesus, knowing that the Father had given everything into his hands and that he had come from God and was going to God ...". This picks up the similar phrase of verse 1, and is rendered necessary by the mention of Judas and the action of the devil. As always, Jesus is in command of the situation: he knows what is going to happen and is prepared to deal with it. He knows moreover his origin and his destination. The incarnation is part of the divine drama and it reaches its conclusion in the passion which is also the moment of the resumption of his glory. The three main verbs of verse 4 (he rises; he lays aside; he girded) describe Jesus' actions at the supper, for which the participles of the preceding verses have been setting the scene. His laying aside his garments and his girding of himself with a towel describe the meaning of the whole of the incarnation, his coming from God and his going to God (cf Marsh 1968:484f). In this act we are given a vivid description in the form of a story of the meaning of Philippians 2:6-8 – he who is in the form of God emptied himself and took the form of a slave, being made in the likeness of men. What Paul describes in his hymn is set forth in the dramatic action of the foot-washing. It is to be noted that John uses the common verb *tithenai* (lay aside, lay down) in the sense of laying down one's life, with particular reference to Jesus (10:11,15,17f; 15:13; cf 13:37f). The laying aside of his garments illustrates the meaning of the incarnation, culminating in the cross. The action of girding himself with a towel is rather oddly reported in the aorist tense (*diezosen*) following the present *egeiretai* (he arises) and *tithesi* (he lays aside). In this way John lets it be known that this is the really significant event – the incarnation of the Word and all that is involved in his act of service.

The narrative continues with the account of Jesus' washing of the disciples' feet and his drying them with a towel which is the mark of his servanthood. This is a description of the service which the incarnate Son renders to those who are his own (v1). The end of the act of service is marked in verse 12 by the resumption of his clothes, corresponding to the exaltation described in Philippians 2:9-10. The pattern of the narrative of the foot-washing corresponds to the whole of the condescension and exaltation of the Son of God, who came down from heaven (6:38) to give life to the world (6:33) and who is exalted in glory in and through his offering (12:32,34).

Now, the context of this account of the service of the Lord is the Last Supper. Deliberately so, since John wishes to show by this that the meaning of the eucharist instituted at the Last Supper is to be found only in the whole historical act of God in Christ: this was his act of service, and it is this act of service as a whole which is made present and celebrated at every eucharist. That this was John's intention seems to be confirmed by Luke 22:24-27. Luke appears deliberately to have changed the context of the dialogue about greatness and privilege as reported in Mark 10:35-45. In Mark the ambitious strivings of the disciples are contrasted with the humble service of Christ (10:33f) shortly before his entry into Jerusalem. Luke omits the pericope at this point and includes a similar dialogue immediately following the Last Supper. It would almost seem as though John 13:1-11 were providing a midrash on Luke 22:27 – "For who is greater? The one who reclines at a meal or the one who serves?". It has been frequently pointed out that Jewish slaves were not required to perform the menial act of foot-washing. The action of Jesus, the true Jew, is one further way of showing the amazing humility and condescension of the Word of God in his incarnation and self-giving on the cross. Every celebration of the eucharist proclaims this act of service and recalls and makes present the generosity of the Lord.

The service of Christ is directed towards his disciples (v5). They are "his own" of verse 1 to whom he shows the extent of his love. In washing their feet and drying them with the towel he shows that there is no aspect of service which he foregoes. The mark of discipleship is the readiness to accept the service offered: Simon Peter, like many a disciple, shows reluctance. He fails to see that the true dignity of Jesus the Lord is to be discerned in the humble service of the foot-washing. Its connection with the cross is made clear in the words of Jesus (v7) "What *I* am doing *you* do not know now, but you will know afterwards". The meaning of the cross is made clear only in the resurrection, because it is the resurrection which finally shows that Jesus is indeed the eternal Word of God. In the same way, the meaning of the supper is to be found only in the completed act of Christ which culminates in the resurrection.

The language of verses 6 to 10 is baptismal language. To be washed is to be baptized. But John is using such language to express the meaning of baptism rather than to stress its liturgical status. To be baptized is to accept the service and ministry of

Christ the Lord. It also means to participate in the life of Christ (v8), which means too, as the sequel makes clear (vv14-17), to share in his self-giving love and death. In these words then John is expressing the meaning of baptism as the way in which the disciple receives the love and service of Christ and at the same time commits himself to the Lord in loving obedience. Peter's protestations, when he realizes what is involved, show his eagerness to be fully part of Christ by being washed all over. The reply of Jesus is probably to be interpreted to mean that one baptism is sufficient: frequent lustrations, as were practised at Qumran, are unnecessary.

Lest however anyone should think of baptism as a kind of magical charm which operates automatically there is added verse 10b "And you are clean, but not all of you". The only guarantee of faithful discipleship is faithful perseverance. This seems to reflect the covenantal nomism of Judaism, so thoroughly investigated by Sanders (1977:esp 147ff), who shows that in Judaism Israel was chosen by God's free grace, and that the maintenance of this position of g. ace was assured by faithful observance of the Torah. The Christian is maintained in God's grace by his persevering in the love and service of Christ. The various readings in verse 10 do not affect the general picture: the language is baptismal language, but the reference is to the meaning of baptism. This is made clear by the reference to the traitor in verse 11. Judas was chosen by the Lord and united to him in the supper. Yet he betrayed the Lord and was lost (17:12). In this narrative, as Cullmann has pointed out (1953:107), baptism is associated with the eucharist. Both sacraments, though in different ways, are in mind, since each demonstrates the foundation of the Christian life as being the incarnation, death and resurrection of Jesus.

Goulder (1982) sees John 13 as deliberately replacing the institution of the eucharist by an acted parable setting forth the meaning of baptism. He appeals to the custom of washing the feet of the newly baptized as practised at Milan in the time of Ambrose (*Sacr* 3.1:4-7; *Myst* 6:31f). But the meaning of the rite as given by Ambrose is not that envisaged in John 13. In Ambrose it is allegorized so as to refer to the way in which the words spoken to the serpent in Genesis 3:15 ("You shall bruise his heel" – RSV) are annulled through baptism.

It is sometimes argued (e g Lyonnet 1974:231) that Judas did not partake of the eucharist, and that (according to John) the institution of the eucharist took place after Judas had left. The glorification of the Son of Man described in verse 31 is then seen as the moment of the institution of the eucharist, which is explained by the giving of the new commandment in verses 34 and 35. Lyonnet shows clearly enough the connection in meaning between the commandment (with its Old Testament background) and the eucharist. It is however much more likely that John took for granted the fact that the eucharist was instituted at the Last Supper, and deliberately replaced the account of its institution by the narrative of the foot-washing. In this way he drew attention to the meaning of the eucharist and its reference to the whole of Jesus' act of service and love, with its culmination on the cross.

Verse 12b proceeds to explain the meaning of Jesus' action – "Do you know what I have done for you?". The perfect *pepoieka* (I have done) seems to be used deliberately, to stress the real meaning of the action of Jesus. He had now resumed his clothes and sat down. The act is complete, and its meaning is now further developed. The "for you" (*humin*) in verse 12 refers to the disciples of every age who have accepted the service of Christ their Lord. Thus the perfect tense is especially appropriate. Christ's act of self-giving love is for the hearer of the gospel as well as for the twelve. Those who have accepted his service, signified by their baptism, are now obliged to follow him and his example.

In verse 13 Jesus accepts the title *kurios* from those who have received his service. It has already been noted that the title *kurios* (lord) is very rarely used (in other cases than the vocative, when it can be rendered "sir") in the fourth gospel outside chapters 20 and 21, where it occurs nine times. It looks as though John (like Mark and Matthew) wanted to stress that the title rightly belonged to Jesus only after the cross and resurrection. It is found in 6:23 and 11:2, both of which may be connected with the activity of the risen Lord with his people. Jesus' acceptance of this title on the eve of the Passion is a further indication of the way in which this incident refers both to the Passion and to the risen Lord worshipped by the church. As a result those who are now sharing in his life are called to share in his service. For acceptance of him as Lord involves obedience to him. This is what both baptism and eucharist are all about: they are meeting-places of the service of God in Christ to human beings and their responsive obedience to God. What has happened to the Lord is to be reproduced in the disciple, for Christian discipleship is primarily a call to commitment and service, not to privilege and power. Verses 15 to 17 express the meaning of baptism and eucharist: the example of the Lord is to be followed by his disciples. As baptism declares both Christ's love and the believer's obedience, so the eucharist is the opportunity for the renewal of Christ's love and of the disciple's commitment. This commitment is to be reflected in life. As in Judaism, liturgy and life hang closely together.

In verse 18, in true Johannine manner, the theme already touched upon in verses 10 and 11 is resumed. The appalling nature of the breach of the unity secured by the sharing of a meal is shown by the quotation from the psalms. The Greek version of Psalm 41:9 talks of "the man of my peace (*ho anthropos tes eirenes mou*, Heb *'îs šelômî*) on whom I set my hope, who eats my bread" as him who "lifted his heel against me". "The man of my peace" is especially the one who has entered into the peace and reconciliation won by Christ (Jn 14:27; 20:20f) as declared at every eucharist. Disciples could scarcely fail to pick up the allusion. Indeed, verse 20 may well refer to the president of the eucharist, as representing the Lord himself. Certainly Ignatius refers to the *episkopos* as being the type of God (*Mag* 6:1; *Tral* 3:1) or as the representative of Jesus Christ (*Tral* 2:1). For him the *episkopos* is specially the president of the eucharist – "Let that be considered a valid eucharist which is under the bishop or one to whom the bishop entrusts it" (*Smy* 8:1); "It is not permissible either to baptize or to celebrate an *agape* apart from the bishop" (*Smy* 8:2). To see this reference in verse 20 causes an otherwise apparently independent saying to fit closely into the context.

In any case, John, like Luke (22:24-34), contrasts the determination of Jesus to continue on his way with the treachery of

Judas, one of the twelve. John stresses this particularly by his description of Jesus' giving to Judas the choice morsel after dipping it (13:26). Judas is the only one who is explicitly described as receiving any food from the hands of Jesus: after receiving it "Satan entered him" (v27). Certainly there is no indication here that receiving food from the hands of Jesus is in itself a guarantee either of faithfulness or of salvation. John goes on to show more clearly than the synoptics that the treachery harms Judas more than Jesus, for Jesus always knows what is to happen and is always in control. Judas, in leaving Jesus, leaves the light of the world and goes out into the darkness of night (v30). The three monosyllables used (*en de nux* – it was night) mark the solemn conclusion to the meal.

The scene is now fully set for the glorification: the traitor has gone and everything is set in motion for the arrest and the crucifixion. The use of the aorist in verse 31 would seem to imply that the glorification had already taken place because Jesus had definitely committed himself to show his love to the full (v1). In verse 33 Jesus repeats words which he had used to the Jews in different circumstances – "where *I* am going *you* cannot come" (7:33f; 8:21). Now they are spoken to the disciples and linked to the giving of the new commandment the observance of which is to mark the disciples as disciples of Jesus and to assure them that their Lord is with them. Just as the eucharist is the continual setting forth of the love of Christ, so too it is the way in which the mutual love of Christians is displayed and deepened (cf Lyonnet 1974:236f). Loving one another, says Paul (1 Th 4:9), is so fundamental for the Christian that it does not need mentioning. Here in the gospel it is rightly set forth as the basis of the Christian life. But it proceeds from the love of Christ, or from the love of God shown in Christ. So "the love of God" forms part of a liturgical phrase (2 Cor 13:13), and the kiss of love (1 Pet 5:14) is the expression of God's love shown to one another in worship, presumably especially at the eucharist. The presence of Jesus is to be withdrawn from the disciples, but in so far as they show love they will still be known as his disciples and by their love his presence will be kept alive in the world. This theme is carried on in the subsequent discourses (15:1-8; 17:26), already anticipated in 13:20.

What we therefore seem to have in chapter 13 is a vivid description of Jesus' act of loving service to those who are his, in a context which can scarcely fail to remind the hearers of the Last Supper and the institution of the eucharist, and so help them realize that the meaning of Jesus' service is continually proclaimed in every eucharist, where at the same time the disciples are called to reaffirm their allegiance to the Lord by following in their life the same service of love.

The Johannine community: John 15:1-17

The context

Chapters 13 to 17 present a remarkably unified theological theme, in spite of the apparent break at the end of chapter 14, where it looks as though the next stage should be the journey to the garden across the Kedron (18:1). It may be that there were several different discourses or homilies being used in the Johannine community, and that chapters 15 and 16 were originally independent discourses and chapter 17 an independent prayer attributed to Jesus. Chapters 15 to 17 were then appropriately inserted at this point by the final editor, who knew what he was doing. There is no manuscript evidence for the omission of these chapters from the final form of the gospel.

Chapter 14 starts abruptly as an independent piece of writing, so that it is no wonder that the Western text adds an introduction – "And he said to his disciples". In this chapter in the setting of the Last Supper Jesus talks of his comings and goings. Verses 2 to 4 seem to refer to the Parousia, but in verse 3 the present tense is used – "I am coming again". Though this can indeed have a future reference, perhaps there is a deliberate ambiguity with reference to the coming of the Lord in the present in the eucharist which thereby becomes an anticipation of the future Parousia. The belief that such an ambiguity is deliberate may be strengthened by the use of the future "I shall take you to myself" in the same verse. "Come, Lord" (*Marana tha*) is the cry of God's people assembled for worship (1 Cor 16:22; Rev 22:20). It refers equally to the coming of the Lord in the eucharist and at the Parousia. It is for this reason that Aune (1972:101) can say that "the cultic worship of the Johannine community provided a present experience of the exalted and living Jesus in terms of the recurrent actualization of his future Parousia".

Aune (1972:102) believes that although the eucharist was not central for John "the cultic community was the locus for realized eschatology". This would explain the enigmatic references to Jesus' going and coming not only in chapter 14 but also in chapters 15 and 16: the future coming of the Lord is anticipated in the present as the result of the coming of the Holy Spirit, whose function is to make present the risen and ascended Lord amid his people in their worship. It is because of this cultic setting of the gospel that such matters as worship, sacraments and ministry "do not receive explicit treatment precisely because they are the presuppositions of the ecclesial context out of which the gospel arose" (Aune 1972:73).

Chapter 14 goes on to draw out the relationship and unity between the Son and the Father, so that Jesus can say "If you have come to know me, you will know my Father too" (14:7). The theme of abiding (*menein*), so prominent in John, occurs in 14:10, with the description of the Father as abiding in the Son. This is followed in verse 17 by the assurance of the abiding of the Spirit in the disciples – "He abides with you and will be in you". Some important manuscripts (P^{66*} B D* W) here read the present "is in you". Although John is presumably concerned with the disciples of his day, so that the present would certainly be appropriate, it is likely that the future should be read in each case – "He will abide with you and will be in you". The scribal alteration to the present would therefore be explained by the realization that the abiding of the Spirit in the church was a present reality. The form of the word meaning abide (*menei*) can be either future or present, depending on its accentuation, which was not marked in the earliest manuscripts. In verse 20 the mutual indwelling of the Father and the Son is explicitly paralleled by the mutual indwelling of the Son and the disciples. This indwelling is achieved (from the side of the disciples) by keeping Christ's commandments and by loving him, as a result of which (v23) the Father and the Son will come to make their abode (*mone*, the noun formed from the verb *menein*) with them.

In this chapter, as so often in the fourth gospel, there is considerable repetition, but each repetition of a theme contains a new idea. So verse 25 ("These things have I spoken to you while abiding with you") implies that he will no longer be abiding with them, but the next verse makes it clear that the coming of the Holy Spirit will teach the disciples everything and "will bring to your mind all that I said to you".

The short section 14:27-31 has all the signs of the end of a discourse: Jesus is going, but he assures his disciples of his peace – not the ordinary greeting, *šalôm*, but real peace which is the result of reconciliation with God, and therefore leads to a person's integrity and wholeness. The clue to understand this has already been given: the Spirit is to be another paraclete, or counsellor (v16). He will remind (*hupomnesei*) the disciples not simply by recalling Jesus' words as a record of the past, but by making them present and active for the believing disciple. The coming of the Spirit is therefore almost the same as the coming of Jesus (cf 14:16,18). It is not therefore surprising that the invocation of the Spirit (*epiklesis*), even if it did not form part of the earliest liturgical tradition, "was widespread during the most creative period of liturgical formulation" (von Allmen 1969:31). Possibly, in the first century, as von Allmen suggests, the prayer *Marana tha* took the place of the *epiklesis* of the later eastern liturgies. In the fourth gospel, however, the coming of the Lord is dependent on the coming of the Spirit, for it is only in the presence of the Spirit that the presence of the Lord is experienced.

The final words of the chapter – "Arise, let us go from here" (14:31) can be taken in another way. "Arise" (*egeiresthe*) is regularly used to describe the resurrection of Christ (Jn 2:22; Rom 6:9) or the resurrection of Christians (Jn 12:1,9; Eph 5:14), while *agomen enteuthen* (let us go on from here) can refer to the next stage of an argument. Perhaps they may be regarded as an invitation to disciples – "Enter on the new life, and let us see where we go from here".

In any case 14:31 marks the end of a section which starts with 13:1. The themes of this section are to be resumed and re-stated in chapters 15 to 17. It is therefore not surprising that chapter 15 in true Johannine manner refers back to, and builds on, what has been said in chapter 13. Chapter 13 is an acted parable explaining the meaning of the incarnation and of the rite by which this was remembered, proclaimed and made present. The meaning of this – which in effect is the whole content of the gospel – is then further expounded in the whole section 13:12 to 17:26, with its two sub-sections, 13:12 to 14:31 and 15:1 to 17:26. The whole is set in the context of the Last Supper, so that it has the character of a classical symposium, where matters of life and death are discussed around the supper-table.

The true vine

The beginning of chapter 15 uses various techniques to connect the chapter with chapter 13 and to reinforce the context of the supper. So the word *katharos* (clean) is used in John only at 13:10-11 and at 15:3. In 13:10-11 the cleansing is due to the act of Jesus, though in spite of what Jesus has done Judas still intends to pursue his traitorous plans. In 15:3 the cleansing is described as being due to the word (*logos*) of Jesus, for it is through the gospel, the word, which is Christ himself, that cleansing is achieved. Similarly the command to love one another occurs first in 13:34 and is taken up again in 15:12,17. The theme of Jesus' choice of his disciples is found in 13:18 and in 15:16,19. The only other use of the verb "to choose" (*eklegesthai*) is at 6:70 where, as in 13:18 and perhaps implicitly in 15:16,19, the reference is to the contrast between the loyal disciples whom Jesus has chosen and those who, like Judas, betray him. Again, in 15:20 ("A slave is not greater than his master") there is a deliberate reference back to the same saying in 13:16. By such techniques John links chapter 15 to the description of the supper and its meaning in chapter 13.

Not only are there signs of a deliberate connection between chapters 13 and 15. There are also, as many writers have pointed out (e g Braun 1970:23), clear similarities between chapters 6 and 15. In 6:32, at the start of the discourse on the bread of life, Jesus talks of the true bread (*ton arton ton alethinon*) which he then explains to be himself (6:35). In 15:1 Jesus describes himself as the true vine (*he ampelos he alethine*). He, the vine, as the source of true drink is paralleled by the remarks in 6:55 – "my flesh is true (*alethes*) food and my blood is true (*alethes*) drink". The theme of abiding in Christ in 6:56 recurs in 15:4-7, with the stress on abiding in the vine. In 6:51 Jesus asserts "The bread which I shall give is my flesh for (*huper*) the life of the world", while in 15:13 he says "Greater love has no-one than this, that a man lay down his life for (*huper*) his friends", where "his friends" are those who by their obedience show their faith in him and for whom Jesus' death avails. The word *huper* is used by John especially with reference to Jesus' death on behalf of those who are his (6:51; 10:11,15; 11:50,51,52; 17:19; 18:14), and the self-giving love of Jesus is deliberately contrasted with the action of Peter, a representative of "faithful" disciples, in 13:37-38 by the use of similar language.

The eucharist from the earliest times was among other things the outward expression of the unity of believers through their sharing each in the life of Christ. They formed a *koinonia*, a community. Because they each shared in Christ they had become *koinonoi* (participants) of Christ (1 Cor 10:16-18), and this was effected by the Spirit (1 Cor 12:13) so that the church could even be called the *koinonia* of the Holy Spirit (2 Cor 13:13), a phrase which can indicate both the participation in the Spirit and the community which results from it. This was certainly Paul's view, and may even be reflected in Acts 2:42.

It has often been claimed that John 15 is concerned not with the church, but with individuals who are by faith made branches of the vine which is Jesus the risen Lord (Schweizer 1959:235). There is a certain truth in this view, since faith and commitment, which are stressed by John as the foundation of Christian discipleship, have to be expressed personally and individually. But the result of the expression of faith is to find oneself in a community. This is just as we should expect, since it was recognized among both Hebrews and Greeks that the true and full nature of a human being is realized only in community. Life in community with others is the essential context for self-discovery. The nature or form of the community however in which a person lives makes all the difference. The fourth gospel claims that true human community is found through unity in and with Christ, and is expressed by love of the brethren, which means love for fellow-members of the Christian community, as Quispel has decisively demonstrated (1970).

John describes this community as one in which the members are united with one another because each is joined to Christ. So they declare their faith in, and love for, Christ by keeping his commandment to love one another. This was indeed the mark of many an early Christian community, as witnessed to even by that vehement opponent of Christianity, the emperor Julian, who complained that he could not get his followers to show the same love and concern for others as was practised among Christians (Greenslade 1948:23). Earlier on Tertullian drew attention to the remarks of pagans about Christians – " 'See' they say, 'how they love one another' " (*Apol* 39:7). Quispel therefore points out (1970:93) that "Christianity was the only mystery religion with social implications", since the love shown by Christians meant primarily active charity. This understanding of love was clearly expressed in 1 John 3:17-18.

Now in John 15 the vine is Jesus, not the church. The abrupt beginning, without any conecting particle, as at the beginning of chapter 14, is perhaps meant to mark the solemnity of the discourse. It used to be generally held that the metaphor of the vine referred to Israel in view of the many Old Testament passages in which it is so used (Is 5; Ps 80:8-16; Jer 2:21; Ezk 17:6). Jesus therefore is here presented as the true Israel, demonstrating in his life what Israel had been chosen, but failed, to be. Sandvik however (1967:324-325) believes that the imagery refers especially to the Temple. He draws attention to a number of factors to support his view: firstly, Josephus (*Ant* 15:395; *BJ* 5:210) and Tacitus (*Hist* 5:5) describe the golden vine at the entrance of the Herodian Temple; secondly, the Talmud (*Sukka* 49a) identifies the vine of Isaiah 5 with the Temple; and finally he notes the liturgical references in Mark 14:25 ("Truly I tell you, I shall no more drink of the fruit of the vine until that day when I drink it new in the Kingdom of God"), and in Didache 9:2 ("the holy vine of David your servant") and 10:2 ("We thank you, holy Father, for your holy name which you have made to dwell in our hearts"). He concludes that the references to the vine in the Didache and in Mark refer to the Christian community in which the person of Christ replaces the Temple as the focal point of worship, so that the community of believers becomes the new Temple. The language of John 15 of abiding in the vine would be in conformity with such a view. Schnackenburg (1982:106) likewise notes the common use of the symbol of the vine on coins, tombs, ossuaries and lamps, and doubts whether the reference in John 15 is directly to Israel.

In spite, however, of the rich symbolism of the vine in ancient society generally, as will be indicated further below, the language of John 15 seems primarily to refer to Israel. The allusion which John would seem to expect his readers to recognize is surely to Jeremiah 2:21, where the Septuagint reads: "I planted you as a fruit-bearing vine altogether genuine" (*ampelon karpophoron pasan alethinen*). Jesus is himself the new Israel. This reference might well be supported by Psalm 80, where verses 8 to 16 refer to the vine as Israel, and verse 17 (LXX 79:18) has: "Let your hand be upon the man of your right hand and upon a son of man (*huion anthropou*) whom you made strong for yourself." The connection between Israel as the vine and the phrase "son of man" helps pave the way for the identification of Jesus with Israel, and hence for the image of Jesus as the vine. Jesus as the vine cannot be understood without his branches. He is the whole vine, not just the stock, and just as there cannot be a vine without branches, so too the life of the branches depends on their remaining united to the vine. So the theme of abiding (*menein*), already anticipated especially in chapter 14, is here elaborated.

In this respect one can note the resemblance between John's image of the vine and Paul's understanding of the church as the body of Christ. Paul's image refers not to a group or body of people, but primarily to the person of Christ himself who is now made manifest in those who are united to him. For this reason the image of the body of Christ is closely related to Paul's favourite description of the Christian as being "in Christ". This indicates the same sort of relationship between the Lord and believers as is envisaged in John's image of the vine and the branches. In both cases what is being considered is not an organized church structure so much as a community of those who are united with the Lord. In this respect Schneider (1951:142) quite rightly asserts that any witness to Jesus Christ is unthinkable apart from the community or congregation (*der Gemeinde*). In Johannine terms the branches which abide in the vine both share in the life of Christ and bear witness to him by bearing fruit.

How is the abiding in the vine to be realized and expressed? Sandvik (1967:327) has no doubt that the connection with the eucharist is inevitable, and Schnackenburg (1982:108) believes that the final redaction of the gospel involved giving to an original saying of Jesus "a special tone for the community's celebration of the Eucharist and a new meaning". Borig (1967:252) in his very careful analysis of John 15:1-10 rightly stresses that the primary meaning of the vine image, like all the *ego eimi* (I am) sayings, is christological, and that the reference to the eucharist which is clearly there is not a direct one. This is the typical way in which John presents his portrait of Jesus. In talking about Jesus he uses language which reminds his hearers that they, like the original disciples, are to abide in the Lord, and that this abiding is expressed liturgically in the eucharist. It is therefore of interest to note that wine was often poetically and liturgically described as the blood of the grape (Gen 49:11; Dt 32:14; Sir 39:26; 50:15), so that it was an appropriate symbol for the death of Jesus on behalf of his own. By sharing in the eucharist believers share in the death of Jesus, and are thereby linked not only to the risen Lord but also to the first disciples.

Schneiders (1977:229,233) draws attention to the power of the image of the vine as lying in "the identity of nature and life between a vine and its branches", and then goes on to say that "in John all believers are 'first generation' Christians because they are directly generated by the Father in the Spirit as participants in the filiation of the Son. In this respect, then, all Christians are participants in the eye-witness experience". This provides a good example of the use of symbolism in the fourth gospel, the meaning of which would be apparent to those who were already within the Johannine community and who found this experience expressed in the eucharist.

If we remember that the indirect method of theological discourse is the most effective, since it leads the hearers or readers to discover for themselves the meaning which is below the surface, then John's way of proceeding is entirely intelligible. He is not, says Schneider (1951:139), a churchly writer (*kirklicher Schriftsteller*), but he is a man of church praxis: he stands in the congregation and wants to serve it. This is just the right emphasis. John is not interested in the sacraments in themselves, but he is concerned with the person of Jesus, crucified and ascended, and with those who have been given life in him. So his description of Jesus' work is given in terms which help the believers to see the eucharist as the focal point of the whole salvation event which is there made present (cf Klos 1970:69,101).

The eucharist however is no automatic ticket to salvation, as is shown especially in 15:2,6. The cutting off of unfruitful branches is to be interpreted with reference to Judas, who is always mentioned (implicitly or explicitly) in connection with the Last Supper, which is described in 1 Corinthians 11:23, and in all early liturgies, as happening on the night "in which he was being handed over". Judas therefore becomes the symbol of those who do not keep Jesus' commandment and who thereby are excluded from the fellowship and community which the Lord has established through his death and resurrection. The opposite to the response of Judas is the response made by faith in, and commitment to, the Lord, which involves obedience to Christ's commands. Through their faith people become children of God (1:12), sharing in the sonship of Jesus the risen Lord. The expression of faith is made in baptism and renewed in every celebration of the eucharist. The sacraments in the fourth gospel, far from being opposed to faith, in fact presuppose it (Klos 1970:43).

There are other reasons for thinking that John 15 cannot be dissociated from a eucharistic context. Goodenough (1956:100-111) notes the many instances, attested not only in pagan sources but also in Jewish inscriptions, where the vine appears in connection with a chalice. He notes the important position occupied by the symbolic picture of the vine in the synagogue at Dura-Europos, where it was placed above the niche which served as the shrine for the Torah. He believes that the vine was an accepted symbol of long standing, and explains (1956:111) all the varied evidence by the hypothesis that among the Jews from the first century BC onwards "a wine-drinking ritual was at that time of great importance in a mystic hope for the experience of God and for immortality". Although much of the evidence comes from a later period, the golden vine at the Temple shows the importance of the symbolism. The primary reference in John 15:1-10 is to Jesus as the embodiment of Israel, but "fruit" (*karpos*) in this context can scarcely fail to remind hearers and readers of the wine of the eucharist in view of the Markan description of wine as "the product of the vine" (Mk 14:25 – *to genema tes ampelou*). If Jesus, rather than the church, is the vine, then he is the supplier of wine, as he demonstrated at Cana.

The commandment to love one another springs from the love which Jesus himself displayed – "Love one another as I have loved you" (v12). The GNB, alone of English versions, renders the Greek "as I love you", which is a possible translation of the aorist tense used in this instance. The usual rendering, however, is to be preferred, drawing attention to the love of Jesus exhibited on the cross. The command to bear fruit is the command to love, a love which is to be shown to the members of the community united with the Lord. The sense of community in Christ is expressed in cultic acts which mark the believers off from the world. So Grundmann (1959) holds that the true meaning of the commandment to love is expressed most clearly in the giving of the bread and wine to the disciples.

According both to Paul and the synoptics, at the Last Supper Jesus blessed his cup of wine and gave it to the disciples, and in this way he both gave his blessing to the disciples and indicated the unity which they enjoy with their Lord. Grundmann (1959:64) finds it most significant that they drank from a single cup rather than from individual cups, as was usual at Passover. Jeremias (1966:69-70) however believes that as there were objections in the second century to the practice of drinking from a single cup, "it must ... be regarded as most probable that the *earlier custom* was to share *one common cup* at the passover meal, at least in the case of the cup of blessing ..." (italics original). This seems to reflect the position described in the New Testament. The eucharistic context therefore brings out the full meaning of 15:13-16, where verse 13 ("Greater love has no-one than this, that a man lay down his life for his friends") might well be seen as the Johannine equivalent of the Pauline "This is my body which is for you" (*to soma to huper humon* – 1 Cor 11:24). Once again we find John writing the story of Jesus in terms which expound the meaning of the cultic acts of the community.

This understanding is supported by the contrast in verse 19 between the disciples and the world, and between disciples and unbelievers in verses 23 to 25. The eucharist, with the life which flows from it, becomes in sociological terms a boundary-marker. Here is the new community constituted by Christ through his death which recognizes in its worship not only the fellowship or *koinonia* which it enjoys with the Lord and among all its members but also its difference from the unbelieving world.

In order however that this should not be regarded as a voluntary association, John makes it clear that their choice is due entirely to the grace and the call of Christ (15:16). Further, the metaphor of the vine occurs between the two references to the promised coming of the Spirit. It is as though the Spirit is meant to be seen as the guarantee of the risen Lord's presence with his people (14:16-18) and as the interpreter of Jesus' words and actions (15:26; 16:13-15). The members of the Johannine community are thereby helped to see the meaning of their worship under the guidance of the Spirit whose presence is assured to them.

7

Liturgy and life II:
The Passion Narrative

Neither baptism, nor the remission of sins, not
knowledge, not participation in the sacraments, not
the holy table, not the enjoyment of the body, not
the communion in the blood – not one of these
things will be able to be of any benefit to us, unless
we lead an upright and amazing life, freed from
every sin.

John Chrysostom *In Apostolicum Dictum 'Nolo vos
ignorare ...' (1 Cor 10:1)* 6 (*PG* 51:250)

Introduction

From the beginning of the gospel the theme of the cross has
always been in the foreground. Christians would have known
that Jesus' life ended in apparent failure with his execution as a
rebel at the hands of the Roman authorities, but they would be
disciples because they knew that this was only part of the story,.
and that Jesus who was killed is the living Lord of the church.
The gospels are concerned to explain the meaning of the cross
without shirking its reality, but showing that it was part of God's
plan for his world from the start. John does this in a specially
impressive manner, showing that the incarnation was no last-
minute attempt by God to remedy an original plan which had

gone awry, but was rather God's way of declaring his presence with, and love for, his people.

John therefore starts the Prologue with his description of the eternal Word of God, (his *logos*, his plan), who came to his own country (or, "his own property" – *eis ta idia*), while those who were his own people (*hoi idioi*) did not receive him (1:11). The reader will have known that not only did they not receive him, but they actually handed him over to the Roman authorities (18:35). This was all part of the divine plan: the eternal Word of God became a human being, and as such became liable to all that accompanies the human condition. His destiny of suffering is one which he freely accepts. So he is the Lamb of God (1:29,36), designated as such at his baptism, and fulfilling his role as the Passover Lamb (19:36 cf Ex12:46) slaughtered to effect the new exodus, the redemption of God's people.

The hour of his death is therefore the hour of his glory: anticipated in 2:4 it reaches its fulfilment in 17:1, but there have been references to it throughout the gospel, and it is first revealed free from any ambiguity in 12:23 – "The hour has come for the Son of Man to be glorified". What first looks like a tragic defeat is seen in the light of its consequences to be a glorious triumph. So at the end of chapter 16 the disciples are encouraged – "Take heart: I have overcome the world". The victory is viewed not only as having already been achieved but as a continuing victory in which the disciples share. It is with such an expression of confidence that we turn to chapter 17, before considering the Passion Narrative itself.

The consecration prayer of Jesus and his disciples: John 17

The chapter has a two-fold function: on the one hand it marks the conclusion of the whole section which started with 13:1, as it summarizes the meaning of the incarnation and the gospel. On the other hand it is a preparation for the Passion Narrative proper, since the consecration of the Son to which it refers is described in the Passion Narrative. The chapter can best be regarded as John's expansion and interpretation of the prayer of Jesus in Gethsemane as recorded in the Synoptics, especially as found in Luke 22:42, in the accepted tradition of Jewish midrash. Certainly the whole prayer is very carefully constructed, as Malatesta (1971) has shown in detail.

There are three main divisions of the prayer: i) verses 1c to 8 where Jesus prays for himself; ii) verses 9 to 19, where Jesus prays for the disciples of his own time; iii) verses 20 to 26, where Jesus prays for future believers. By this structural arrangement, as Minear expresses it (1977:354),

> When they read chapter 17, John's audience would have been reminded of this endless chain of being ... The word which they had heard (17:20) would remind them of the word which their predecessors had heard (17:14, including the beloved disciple), and they would recognize this word as Jesus himself, the word of life and the word of God.

The divisions of the prayer are linked to each other by the recurrence of similar words and phrases. So, for example, the themes of the first section are taken up again in the third, so that verses 25d to 26b (the centre of the third section) correspond to the centre of the first section (v3). In this way we are given not a spontaneous prayer but a deliberately designed composition by which the evangelist presents the significance and purpose of the incarnation. The focus all along is on Jesus, the giver of eternal life, and those who are united with him. The end of the central division of the prayer reaches a christological climax: the word of God is the declaration of God's truth in the person of Jesus (v7b). "Your word is truth" is a quotation from Psalm 119:142, where in the Greek version, according to one manuscript (S), *logos* (word) renders the Hebrew *torah*. Throughout Psalm 119 "word" and "law" are used interchangeably. John is asserting that the centre of unity for God's people is no longer the Torah as the sign of the covenant, but the Word of God made flesh, Jesus Christ, who reveals the truth of life in revealing God.

Just as the purpose of the incarnation was described in the narrative of the foot-washing, so now it is summed up in different and more explicit terms. The participation in Christ, to which reference was made in 13:7-11, is now seen to be the result of Christ's glorification on the cross (17:20-26). This is the purpose of the incarnation, to offer to men and women a share in the eternal life which is found only in union with God.

The prayer of chapter 17 has obvious liturgical overtones. It has many allusions to the Lord's Prayer, and Walker (1982:238) considers that it can best be understood as a "re-working and expansion of the basic themes of the Lord's Prayer in terms of specifically Johannine theology". The following points of resemblance may be noted: Father (*Pater*, v1; cf Lk 11:2); the glorification of the Father by the Son (v1), corresponding to the petition "Hallowed be your name", together with the stress throughout John 17 on the name of God; the prayer for the gift of eternal life (*zoe aionios*, v2), which is the Johannine equivalent of the kingdom of God, as is made clear in 3:3,5,15, so that it resembles "Your kingdom come" of the Lord's Prayer; the prayer for the gift of the knowledge of the Son (v3) is comparable to the petition "Give us this day our daily (*epiousios*) bread", where the meaning of *epiousios* is far from clear. Jesus has already been described as the bread of life (6:48), and *epiousios* may well in fact refer to the person of Christ, as would be suggested by the rendering of the Vulgate *supersubstantialem* (supernatural), or the rendering of the curetonian Syriac "everlasting", in Matthew 6:11. In this connection it should be recalled that there has already been an echo of the Lord's Prayer in 6:34 "Lord, always give us this bread". The prayer for the knowledge of the Father as the only true God and of Jesus Christ (v3) is not so different from, and may be seen as the positive expression of, the petition "Forgive us our sins", especially if the singular form, *ten opheilen* (our debt), as found in Didache 8:2, is read. The knowledge of the Father through the revelation of the Son is the way by which the alienation caused by sin is overcome. The petition in 17:15 is an amplification of the final petition in the Lord's Prayer "deliver us from the evil one" (*tou ponerou*, as in Mt 6:13; Did 8:2).

No doubt the Lord's Prayer, in an Aramaic version, goes back to Jesus himself, and it is likely to have formed part of the earliest Christian liturgies. Certainly Luke 11:1 gives the impression that the Lord's Prayer was meant to be a mark of Christian disciples, just as John's disciples had their own form of prayer. After the resurrection the meaning of the petitions is likely to have changed, so that the eschatological reference which is probably to be found especially in the word *epiousios* (daily) – which some versions render as "tomorrow's bread" – is seen especially in the fourth gospel to have been anticipated in the person of Jesus, without denying a consummation in the future.

But whatever the relation between the Lord's Prayer and John 17 may have been, there is more to be said about the general liturgical background of the chapter. Feuillet (1975:21) describes the atmosphere of the prayer as "heavily eucharistic", though he believes that it is "not directly concerned with the eucharistic mystery". As the culmination of the Farewell Discourses it resembles Moses' farewell song in Deuteronomy 32 and his blessing of the people of Israel in the next chapter. In spite of a certain structural similarity, however, John 17 has been composed in a much more solemn and liturgical form. Bouyer (1966:99-101) compares the prayer to Jewish benedictions (*berakôt*) and notes that thanksgiving and praise form the thread which runs through it. Here is no gloomy prediction of, or meditation on, Jesus' death, but a prayer of thanksgiving for the task entrusted to the Son which he has so faithfully accomplished. Bouyer recognizes the dominant theme as being the divine glory, radiating from the glorification of the Saviour by the cross. On this theme other themes converge – the knowledge of God, the sanctification of those who are his, the giving of life, union in love which is union in the life of God. "These are the thoughts", writes Bouyer, "which the Last Supper would call to mind for the first Christians and which would be sure to have permeated their later eucharistic celebrations" (1966:101, translated).

Rather surprisingly Brown (1970:746-747) has doubts about the eucharistic reference in this chapter, in spite of the admitted similarities between it and Didache 9 and 10 and the belief of Cyril of Alexandria and John Chrysostom that John 17 has the eucharist in mind. Brown notes that "*Didache* IX-X mentions the eucharistic bread and wine, while John XVII does not". This, however, is just what we should expect: Didache is a somewhat enigmatic handbook for Christian preachers and teachers. It therefore gives some explicit instructions about various matters in the life of the church. The fourth gospel cannot explicitly describe the eucharistic celebrations of Christians, since it is concerned with the story of Jesus, and the church's eucharist could take place only after his death and resurrection (cf Thüsing 1970:173). It therefore records the final prayer of Jesus in terms which enable its readers or hearers to recognize that in the eucharistic prayer the believers are joined together with Christ in his constant intercession for them. That this prayer was at the centre of their eucharistic celebration is indicated not only by the Didache (9:1-4) but more clearly by Justin (*Apol* 1:65,67) and Hippolytus (Dix 1968:7-9).

Feuillet (1975:c 2) draws attention to the structural similarity between the Jewish liturgy of the Day of Atonement and the earliest eucharistic liturgies, and especially to the structural similarity between John 17 and the liturgy of the Day of Atonement. Leviticus 16 describes how the High-Priest is to make "atonement for himself, and for his household and for all the congregation of Israel" (v17), corresponding to the three divisions of the prayer in John 17 – for himself, for the first disciples and for all who will believe in him and who form the new Israel. Both in Leviticus and John 17 the first two groups are closely joined together. Feuillet further draws attention to the importance of the name which the Father has given to the Son (vv11-12) and the way in which on the Day of Atonement the High-Priest uttered the otherwise ineffable name of God ten times in the Holy of Holies. He therefore concludes (1975:74):

> Each year, during the festival of atonement, the High Priest entered the holy of holies and restored to Israel its condition as a holy people that was consecrated to Yahweh amid a pagan world. So too, in John 17, Jesus the high priest enters the dwelling of the Father and intercedes with him to keep from sin the new people of God whom Jesus has won by his redemptive sacrifice ...

John writes in the way he does because he is aware of the unity which exists between Christians of his own day and those of the earliest years. "There is no fixed boundary in John's gospel between the Word of Christ and the proclamation (*kerugma*) of the evangelist" (Schneider 1951:139, translated). So there is nothing deceptive in reporting as the words of Christ what springs from the eucharistic worship of the early church, for there in the eucharist of the Christian community the Lord is speaking and praying as surely as he prayed on the night of the Last Supper.

It is this sense of unity between the disciples and their risen Lord which provides a further clue to the eucharistic allusions of John 17. The chapter marks the end of the Farewell Discourses, and recapitulates the themes which occur in them. By its concern with the unity of the disciples with their Lord it emphasizes the theme of chapter 15. But in chapter 15 the stress is on the need of the branches, the disciples, to abide in the vine, the Lord, by keeping his commandments. In chapter 17, on the other hand, the prayer is concerned with the unity which Jesus has with the disciples in the Father. If the eucharistic allusions of chapter 15 lead the disciples to see that the meaning of their worship must be expressed in their life by loving one another, the allusions of chapter 17 provide the assurance that the Lord who is with them in their worship is constantly with them to build them up in unity with each other through their unity with him.

This unity results from the consecration and self-offering of the Lord, which has always been the central reference of the eucharist (1 Cor 11:26) and which is the guarantee of the fulfilment of the prayer of Jesus that all may be one in him. He made known to the disciples the name of God (17:26) thereby revealing the identity of the one whose name could not normally be uttered. The revelation was effected through his life of consecration and self-offering on the cross. But this disclosure of the Father's name is not only in the past. "I shall continue to make it known" he goes on to say. The purpose of this is that the Father's love for the Son may be "in" the disciples, and that the Son himself may be "in" them. The way in which the revelation of God's name is to be continued is in the liturgical act which represents and sets forth the once-for-all sacrifice of Christ, what Paul records in the words of Jesus as being "for my *anamnesis*" (1 Cor 11:24-25). Such an understanding is supported by the words of the prayer that the Father's love, and Christ himself, may be "in" the disciples. This kind of language would most appropriately refer to the eucharist in which the communion (*koinonia*) of the Lord with believers is symbolically and clearly expressed.

The unity described in John 17 is especially the unity of the disciples with their Lord. Perhaps, as Kysar suggests (1977:366), the fourth gospel arose from a Christian school which was struggling to preserve "a distinctive tradition all its own" over against the synagogue, or perhaps, as the first epistle of John indicates, the community had to assert its identity and orthodoxy in the face of those who had seceded from it. In any case, whatever the exact situation may have been, the fourth gospel strongly affirms the need of the unity of the community as a result of the unity of each of its members with Christ. This has always been the understanding of one, if not the most important, aspect of eucharistic worship, as expressed by Justin (*Apol* 1:67; *PG* 6:429), who describes how after the eucharist "we continually remind one another of these things, and those of us who can provide aid to those in need". He goes on to talk of the more general rendering of aid to orphans, widows, the sick, the distressed, prisoners, foreigners and all who are in any kind of need. This more comprehensive description derives from the command to love one another, which in the fourth gospel, as has already been mentioned, referred to the mutual love of disciples, and which Justin sees as especially important.

The same theme of unity is expressed more rhetorically in a later age by John Chrysostom, who constantly refers to the meaning of the eucharist in terms of unity. He pays special attention to Judas as the type of those who betray their Lord and break the unity signified by the eucharist. Talking of the greeting of peace at the eucharist, he said:

> Let us then continually remember, I pray you, these words and the most awesome greeting of one another. For this greeting binds our hearts together and causes us all to be one body and limbs of Christ, since we all in fact share in the one body. Let us then truly become one body, not by mingling our bodies with one another, but by knitting our souls to one another in the bond of love. (*De prod Iud* 2:6; *PG* 49:391)

These words of Justin and of Chrysostom would seem to be a perfectly fair development of the themes of John 15 and especially of chapter 17.

The unity however needs to be more fully described, if we are to be faithful to the fourth gospel. It is unity in the glory of Christ (17:22), and the glory of Christ in John is to be found on the cross. So the unity of the disciple with his Lord is a unity in suffering. In this respect it is similar to the narrative in Mark 10:37-39 when James and John do not realize what they are asking, since those on the right and left hand of Jesus, lifted on the cross, are the crucified brigands. So the prayer of Jesus in John 17 is similar to the Lord's demand in the synoptics – "Whoever wishes to be my disciple, let him deny himself and take up his cross and follow me" (Mk 8:34), where the Greek for "deny" and "take up" is in the aorist tense in each case, indicating the need for a moment of active decision, whereas the verb "follow" is expressed in the present to show the ongoing nature of discipleship.

The unity in glory is therefore described further in terms of the Lord's consecration. He consecrates himself on behalf of the disciples that they too may be consecrated, made holy (*hagioi*), the regular description of Christians in the New Testament (Rom 1:7). The consecration of Jesus means his death, as is clearly shown by Ignatius (*Eph* 12:2) who describes Paul in his martyrdom as "consecrated" (*hegiasmenos*), the same word as is used of Jesus in John 17:19. Every celebration of the eucharist refers not only to the sacrifice of Christ but also to the sacrifice of Christians. Christ's once-for-all offering is carried on in the church (cf Col 1:24). The description of the eucharist as a sacrifice involves a danger unless it is seen in conjunction with the ongoing sacrifice of Christians who enter into the once-for-all sacrifice of Christ. It is presumably in this sense that Didache 14:1-2 should be understood:

> On the Lord's day of the Lord meet together and break bread and make eucharist (*eucharistesate*), after first confessing your sins, that your sacrifice (*thusia*) may be pure (*kathara*). But if anyone has a dispute with his neighbour, let him not meet with you until they are

reconciled, that your sacrifice may not be defiled.

In John 17, therefore, at the end of the farewell discourses, the meaning of the Passion is made clear. It is a glorious triumph (16:33), being the free declaration of the Father's love for his own: here is the act of God's grace which provides the way for that communion and fellowship with the Father of all who will believe in Jesus the Lord. It is noteworthy that the name "Jesus Christ" appears in the fourth gospel only in 17:3 and 1:17. There is no reason to suspect that this is not deliberate, or that it is an alien intrusion. The name Jesus Christ, as 1 John makes abundantly clear, draws attention to the continuity which exists between the exalted Christ, the anointed one of God, and the historical person of Jesus. In 1:17 it was necessary to state it clearly to underline the claim of 1:14 – "The Word became flesh". In 17:3 likewise, as God's plans for his world are unfolded, the destiny of the disciples is presented as being bound up with the historical Jesus in his suffering and with the risen Christ in glory. In the Passion Narrative he will be described simply as Jesus, but from chapter 20 he is the Lord (*kurios*), the title given to YHWH in the Old Testament, for he is now risen and enjoys the name which is above every name (Phil 2:9). This name which Jesus claims as having been given him by the Father (17:11-12) plays an important part in the argument. Jesus prays that the Father may keep the disciples in his name, and says that he has kept them in the Father's name. As the joint name of the Father and of the Son it is probably to be interpreted with a baptismal reference. So the Lord prays for those who have been baptized "into the name" (*eis to onoma* – Mt 28:19; Did 7:1,3) of Christ or of the Trinity that they may be preserved faithfully in that name and relationship. Once again there is an allusion to Judas (17:12) to remind disciples that neither baptism nor eucharist is a guarantee of salvation. It is always possible to fall away: hence the reason for Jesus' prayer, which assures the future disciples of God's grace and presence with them if only they will persevere in keeping his commandments. Every celebration of the eucharist is both the assurance of God's love in Christ and the renewal of the disciple's commitment to his Lord. On the one hand it is the occasion of thanksgiving (*eucharistia*) for God's grace shown in Christ; on the other, it is the occasion for a renewed expression of faith in the acceptance of God's grace.

In the earliest forms of the eucharistic prayer the *amen* at the end was considered to be of great importance, as signifying the believer's assent to the prayer of the president. It is especially emphasized by Justin, who indicates that it is only after the assent of all the people, expressed by their *amen*, that the distribution of the bread and wine is made. His mention of the people's assent in the *amen* on the only two occasions when he describes the eucharistic prayer (*Apol* 1:65,67) is especially significant. Though the *Apostolic Tradition* of Hippolytus mentions without further ado the *amen* at the end of the eucharistic prayer (Dix 1968:9), the communicant at the Paschal Mass is instructed to say *amen* when receiving the bread and each of the three cups – water, milk, wine (Dix 1968:41-42). The *amen* is found too at the end of the eucharistic prayer in Didache 10:6, where presumably it is meant to be uttered by the people.

Possibly even 1 Corinthians 14:16 refers to the *amen* at the end of the eucharistic prayer: "If you bless (*euloges*) in the Spirit, how will the ordinary worshipper (*idiotes*) be able to say *amen* to your thanksgiving (*eucharistia*)?" The reference here might well be to the celebration of the eucharist by someone speaking in tongues under the inspiration of the Spirit. Certainly *eulogein* (bless) and *eucharistia* (thanksgiving) are both technical terms describing the eucharist, though they can indeed have a wider reference. So too in 2 Corinthians 1:20 – "For all God's promises are 'yes' in him (*sc* Jesus Christ): that is why it is also through him that we say *amen* to his glory". Since this immediately precedes two verses with strong baptismal allusions, the liturgical use of *amen* at the eucharist may well be under consideration here. Perhaps the frequent use of *amen, amen* in the fourth gospel (seven times in cc 13-16) is a further liturgical allusion. Whatever the truth of all this may be, the language of John 17 reminds the reader of his part in the divine drama which has been played out in the cross and resurrection and which is made present in the eucharist.

The references to the eucharist however must not blind us to the real meaning of the prayer. As Hoskyns says, "it would be a grave misunderstanding of his (*sc* John's) purpose to explain this as merely a mystical idealizing of Christian worship" (1947:495). It refers rather to the origin of the Christian community as deriving from the self-offering of Christ in which those who belong to him are called to share, in the assurance that the victory which he has won will also be theirs. It is this victory which the eucharist proclaims.

The Passion Narrative: John 18 & 19

The Passion Narrative in all four gospels seems to have been the first connected narrative of any length known to the earliest disciples. The marked similarity between the account in the fourth gospel and that in the synoptics is here especially significant, in view of the considerable differences which are to be found elsewhere. It has therefore often been suggested that the Passion Narrative was a connected whole from the beginning. If this were so, then it would mean that Mark took the Passion Narrative as an independent unit and added chapters 1-13. This view has been strongly maintained by Trocmé (1975:c 4), who also later (1983:82) argued that the Passion Narrative was originally a liturgical narrative, composed as a "commemoration of Christ's death by Christians during the Jewish Passover celebrations" when they would celebrate not only his death but also his resurrection and his living presence with them.

It is however very difficult to consider Mark's gospel as ever existing independently of his Passion Narrative, and recent studies have made it clear that Mark's Passion Narrative "constitutes a theologically inseparable and homogeneous part of the Gospel whole" (Kelber 1976:157). Although therefore it is very doubtful whether there was a written independent coherent account of the passion of Christ before Mark's gospel, it can be presumed that the story of the trial and crucifixion of Jesus was regularly told among early disciples, since such a story was the basis of their faith. It always included a reference to the last meal of Jesus with his disciples, as well as to the action of Judas. As Donahue (1976:7) puts it: "The growth of the passion traditions is a miniature of the growth of early Christianity as a self-conscious religious group." Such a story would be particularly appropriate in the context of baptism "into Christ's death" (Rom 6:3) and of the eucharist where believers "proclaimed the Lord's death until he should come" (1 Cor 11:26). In any case the story is likely to have been told especially when the disciples met together for worship.

In this respect the Passion Narrative plays a part similar to the Passover *Haggadah*, where the narrative explains the meaning of the meal and the ritual. If this was the origin of the Passion Narrative, it needs to be emphasized that its primary reference is not to any kind of liturgical observance, but to God's act of redemption in Christ which is here described in terms of a historical account. Just as the Passover *Haggadah* told of the redemption of Israel in the exodus, so the Passion Narrative tells of the redemption effected by Christ in terms which express the belief of the Christian community. The narrative assures the community of its origin and its destiny. The different evangelists had each his own interpretation of Jesus' life and death. John's Passion Narrative, therefore, as is to be expected, is coloured by his own theological insights and perceptions. Some, if not all, of these are particularly valuable in helping the congregation to see the significance of their worship, but they do this because they focus the attention of believers on the crucified Lord of the church.

In this way John describes the Passion as a triumphal victory of God's love. Here is the account of the way in which "God so loved the world that he gave his only Son in order that everyone who believes in him should not perish, but have eternal life" (3:16). The aorist tenses (loved, *egapesen*; gave, *edoken*) point to the act of God's love accomplished on the cross. So John's Passion Narrative is closely linked to the life and response of disciples, for they, like Jesus and through him, are those who have come "from above" (8:23; 17:16) and who share in his triumph (16:33).

Jesus is the central figure of the story. All along he is represented as being in control of the situation. Already shown earlier in the gospel, and especially in chapter 17, this attitude is further depicted in chapter 18. In verse 4 he knows of all that is coming upon him, and his reply to those who come to arrest him is made in the ambiguous terms which the readers of the gospel have come to expect – *ego eimi* (v5), meaning both "I am he" and "I am", the divine name. The soldiers' falling to the ground (v6) is the typical response to a divine revelation (Dan 10:9; Mt 17:6; Ac 9:4; Rev 19:10, 22:8). Jesus' attitude of calm control is continued in the following verses: he is ready to drink the cup which the Father has given him (18:11), so that Peter's attempt at resistance is seen as misguided. The teaching which he gives is nothing of which he could be ashamed. The trial before Pilate (18:33-38) becomes almost a trial of the governor by the prisoner who in his own person gives the answer to Pilate's question, "What is truth?" (18:38). John has already (14:6) alerted the reader to understand the irony, but Pilate remains in ignorance.

Jesus meanwhile has expressed before Pilate his own authority and freedom. His seamless robe (19:23) may well symbolize the High-Priest's robe, as described by Josephus and Philo, the latter of whom understood it as a symbol of the *logos* which is "the bond of the universe (*desmos ton hapanton*) which holds everything together" (Barrett 1978:550). Jesus' final words from the cross proclaim his death as a victory, especially if it is regarded in sacrificial terms: "It is accomplished" means that the sacrifice is complete, the task of the Son has been accomplished in triumph, since the goal (*telos*) of his incarnate life has now been achieved. This was the moment when "he handed over the Spirit", which affords a good example of the double meaning of so much of John's writing. The words could simply mean that he died, he gave up his spirit: but in fulfilment of 7:39 they refer to Jesus' glorification on the cross as the prerequisite for the gift of the Spirit to the disciples, which is described more fully in 20:21-23.

The whole account is centred on the person of Jesus, whose death on the cross, his consecration, is the means by which believers find their deliverance through their unity with him. This is exactly the centre of all Christian worship. To help disciples recognize that all their worship, especially as expressed in baptism and eucharist, finds its meaning in the death of Christ, John provides allusions to the Passover which can scarcely be overlooked. Jesus himself is depicted as the Passover Lamb, executed on the cross at the time when the Jews were slaughtering their lambs to celebrate their deliverance from bondage. Such an understanding is clearly indicated by the citation of Exodus 12:46, even though similar words in Psalm 34:20 have a wider reference. So too it is likely that the odd language of John 19:29 – "They surrounded a sponge full of sour wine with hyssop" – has a reference to Passover, and that the suggestion that *husso* (on a javelin) should be read instead of *hussopo* was due to a failure to recognize the allusion to the Passover when hyssop or bitter herbs would have been used.

The reason for Jesus' death has already been indicated in 18:14, where Caiaphas' prediction that Jesus was to die "on behalf of the people (*laos*)" is recalled. He is described in terms of the suffering servant of Isaiah, to whom an explicit reference was made in 12:38, even though there is no such clear reference in the Passion Narrative. So Jesus is given slaps by a servant of the High-Priest (18:22) and by the soldiers (19:3), where it is to be noted that the Greek word for "slap" (*rhapisma*) occurs in the Greek bible only here and in the Passion Narrative of Mark (14:65), and in the Septuagint version of Isaiah 50:6 with reference to the servant of YHWH. Similarly Jesus' silence in 19:9 recalls the servant's silence before his persecutors (Is 53:7) and his crucifixion between two robbers reminds the reader of the servant's fate (Is 53:12).

The story of the piercing of the side of Jesus serves to reinforce the allusions to the worship of the church. The account has occasioned much debate. Whatever else it may mean, it certainly refers to the reality of Jesus' death and true humanity: here is no docetic Christ. Venetz (1976:94), after a careful analysis, concludes that 19:34b-35 was a late redactional insertion which rather confused the theological structure of the pericope 19:31-37. But in view of its agreement with the theology and style of the fourth gospel, Venetz regards it as a written or oral tradition added by the evangelist (the final redactor) to his source. Westcott (1908:284-286) gives the various patristic interpretations, which need not concern us now.

The incident of the lance-thrust not only refers to the reality of

Jesus' death, and therefore to his true humanity, but also witnesses to the Lordship of the exalted Christ. Venetz (1976:100) draws attention especially to the use of the perfect in verse 35 "has borne witness" (as RSV translates *memartureken*). He concludes that this perfect tense in the fourth gospel always refers not to an outward, visible event, but to the person of Jesus himself. It is always a christological statement declaring Jesus to be the Son of God (1:34; cf 3:26; 5:33,37) or one who speaks with the authority and truth of God. The stress on the incident of the lance-thrust shows that the evangelist considered it to be of the greatest importance, and the use of the perfect participle (v35) "he who has seen it" (*ho heorakos*) indicates that the evangelist considers the picture of the pierced Jesus as being an object of continual contemplation, an idea supported by Zechariah 12:10 quoted in verse 37, a text which was used too in Revelation 1:7 where the "one whom they pierced" is he who will come in glory. Since Zechariah 12:10 refers to the one who is contemplated and mourned as the beloved and the first-born (LXX *agapetos, prototokos*), it is not surprising that the New Testament authors found this text fulfilled in Jesus on the cross. The crucified and pierced Jesus is the Lord who is to be seen and contemplated for ever. When Christians celebrate eucharist they believe that this is what they are doing.

The incident of the piercing of Jesus' side is regarded by Malatesta (1977:169) as offering "the most meaningful symbolism in the entire gospel". For although the words refer to the reality of Jesus' death and therefore of his humanity, a secondary reference to baptism and eucharist is to be seen here too, in spite of the unexpected order, "blood and water" (*contra* 1 Jn 5:6). This order may be due to the rabbinic interpretation of Psalm 78:20 – "Moses struck the rock twice, and first it gushed out blood and then water" (*Midrash Rabbah on Exodus*: Burge 1987:94) – or perhaps the order symbolizes the giving of the Spirit, often described in the fourth gospel by the image of water, as being dependent on the death of Christ, symbolized by the blood. John Chrysostom in his *Baptismal Instructions* (Harkins 1963:16-17) is emphatic that the passage refers to baptism and eucharist, and he makes much of the order which he reads, "water and blood", though there is no evidence in the manuscripts for such an order.

Certainly, as Venetz (1976:111) says, any congregation celebrating eucharist and baptism would discover in these verses the source of its faith and life, and even if John did not consciously intend this, Venetz recognizes the legitimacy of such an interpretation. If however, as is most likely, the Christian community for whom the gospel was written was already celebrating baptism and eucharist, such a reference would be inevitable, and the evangelist would be aware of this. If then 19:34b-35 is a later addition by the final editor of the gospel it may well have been added to draw the community's attention to the presence of the crucified Lord among them in their worship.

Malatesta (1977:177) offers guidance applicable not only to this text but to the whole of the gospel:

> ... the only adequate way for a Christian to 'read' the text of John – or of any biblical text – is to see it *both* in its historical-critical sense *and* in the sense given by the theology and contemplation of Tradition, the liturgical prayer of the Church ... and the resonance of the text in the life of the people of God at any given period.

If indeed the primary symbolism of the text is to the gift of the Spirit as a result of the death of Jesus, then the reference to baptism and eucharist as means by which this gift is mediated to believers would seem most natural (cf Thüsing 1970:173). Hoskyns (1947:533) takes a similar view, and refers to Hebrews 9:19, where the reader is reminded that the first covenant was inaugurated with blood and water and hyssop, so that not only the order of words in 19:34 but also the reference to hyssop in 19:29 provide a deliberate allusion to the death of Christ as inaugurating the new covenant between God and his people.

Although the word for covenant (*diatheke*) does not occur in the Johannine literature (except in Rev 11:19, with a reference to "the ark of the covenant"), the idea of the new covenant is everywhere apparent especially in chapters 13 to 17, and is closely connected with the giving of the new commandment. Lyonnet (1974:222-228) draws attention to the allusions to Jeremiah 31:31-34 which are to be found in John 6:45, which he believes are reflected too in John 6:26-29 with the contrast between the works of law and faith. The new covenant is written "in their hearts", so that the language of John 13:34 – "A new commandment I give (*didomi*) to you" – corresponds to the new covenant of Jeremiah which involves a change of attitude rather than the imposition of a new law. The new commandment of John 13:34 is a reminder of the way in which liturgy and life are closely connected. The Christian gospel is not primarily concerned with cultic observance, but with the living of life in community, with ethics. John 19:34 therefore declares the origin of this life to be the death of Jesus, and in so doing he alludes to liturgical practices which bear witness to it and which enable disciples to share in, and display, Christ's life in the world.

Such an understanding is supported by other passages already examined. Thüsing (1970:173) for example draws attention to John 3:5 and 6:51-58, where references to baptism and eucharist seem inevitable. Since the word for "blood" (*haima*) is used elsewhere in John only with a eucharistic reference (other than the plural in 1:13), and since water is often symbolic of the Spirit, the reference here to baptism and eucharist is very likely, though we must remember that the primary meaning of 19:34, as of the Passion Narrative as a whole, concerns the centrality of the crucifixion as providing the way to understand the person and work of Jesus as the exalted Lord. It is from his death and resurrection that the life-giving gift of the Spirit, as of the sacraments, comes.

Although the central character of the Passion Narrative is Jesus himself, the disciples, here as elsewhere in the fourth gospel, are closely involved with him. This has already been clearly indicated in chapters 15 and 17. The Passion Narrative shows how this unity was displayed among the first disciples, and provides both a warning and a promise, as John displays all the irony which the reader has come to expect from him (cf Lindars 1972:535). Jesus and his disciples go together to the garden (18:1), where Judas, one of the twelve, leads his captors. Although John has already underlined the treachery of Judas (13:18), he does not mention that Judas kissed Jesus, perhaps because he does not wish to undermine in any way the solemnity of the kiss of peace exchanged among the disciples in their worship. In Judas we see one of the apostolic band who deliberately breaks the unity for which Jesus prayed. But this is all part of the divine plan, and in accordance with scripture (Ps 41:9).

Peter is the next representative of the disciples introduced into the narrative, and he fulfils Jesus' prediction spoken at the supper (13:38). After a misguided attempt to defend his Lord (18:10-11), he goes with John inside the High-Priest's courtyard. Then there follows the story of the disciple's trial, more closely interwoven than in Mark with the trial of his Lord. Where Jesus perseveres, the disciple fails. Yet Jesus trusts his disciples and assures the High-Priest that those who have heard him can tell the High-Priest what Jesus has been saying. Immediately afterwards Peter once again denies all knowledge of his Lord.

Peter is contrasted in John's account not only with Jesus, but also with the women and the Beloved Disciple who stood at the cross. There the Beloved Disciple takes the place of Jesus as his mother's son (19:26-27). In this way the evangelist dramatically portrays the meaning of Jesus' words of the previous evening (13:20; 15:1-7; 17:26). The unity of Jesus and his disciples is effected through the cross, and the behaviour of Judas, and indeed of Peter, is contrasted with the faithful perseverance of the Beloved Disciple.

The stories of Judas and Peter are presumably reports of what happened: in this sense they are historical. But they are related by John in a way which gives them special significance for disciples of a later time, particularly as they express their faith in Christ and their unity with one another in the eucharist. Lindars, for example, (1972:541) is probably correct to see in the *ego eimi* ("I am") of 18:5 a cross-reference to 13:19 – "Now I tell you before it happens, so that when it happens you may believe that I am (*ego eimi*)". He talks of "the tragic irony of the situation" which the expression would call to mind. But the reference back to the Last Supper, with which Judas is always associated, reminds readers of the gospel of their own situation with Jesus with them in their worship, and because they are united with him in his death, the reference to the cup (*to poterion*) which had been given to Jesus to drink (18:11) reminds them that they too have been given a cup to drink so as to share in the death and victory of Jesus. Will they too be like Judas?

This is the only use of *poterion* (cup) in John. It is used in the synoptics in a general sense (Mk 7:4; 9:41 par; Mt 23:25f par), but also with a special reference to the cup at the Last Supper (Mk 14:23; Mt 26:27; Lk 22:17,20). Paul uses the word only with reference to the Last Supper or the eucharist (1 Cor 10:16,21; 11:25 *bis*,26,27,28). Mark 10:38f (= Mt 20:22f) uses it to refer to Jesus' cup of suffering, but the context suggests a eucharistic allusion. The regular Old Testament usage of the cup as the symbol of God's wrath (Ps 10:6 LXX = Ps 11:6; Ps 74:9 LXX = Ps 75:8; Is 51:17, etc; cf Rev 14:10; 16:19; 17:4; 18:6) is here transformed so that the cup of Jesus' suffering becomes the cup of salvation (Ps 115:4 LXX = Ps 116:13), and those who share in the cup share in Jesus' Passion. It is not therefore surprising that all the gospels mention the cup of Jesus in the account of events leading up to the Passion (Mk 14:36; Mt 26:39; Lk 22:42; Jn 18:11). The occurrence of the image in the synoptics so soon after its use at the Last Supper helps to link the church's eucharist with the Passion. There is every reason to think that John had a similar reference in mind.

Finally we are given the story of Joseph and Nicodemus, those hidden disciples who reveal themselves publicly only after the death of Jesus (19:38-42). Nicodemus is of special interest. In chapter 3 he came to Jesus with a question about the new birth: his response to Jesus' answer is not described, but in the Sanhedrin he later demands a fair hearing for Jesus (7:50-52) and at the cross he declares himself publicly. Both in 7:50 and in 19:39 John takes care that the reader should recall Nicodemus' first encounter with Jesus (3:2). Chapter 19 ends with the description of the burial of Jesus, where Joseph and Nicodemus disclose their discipleship. The passage (19:38-42) is of special interest in view of the stress on the body (*soma*) of Jesus (vv38 *bis*,40). The word *soma* occurs in the fourth gospel only in these verses, in 20:12 and in 2:21 (and in the plural in 19:31). Once again the plain meaning of the text is to describe the way in which the body of Jesus was taken from the cross and placed in the sepulchre. Nicodemus has been introduced by John to show that he has reached the goal of his searching. The stress however on taking the body of Jesus, especially in verse 40 where the verb *elabon* (they took) is the word used in connection with the institution of the eucharist (Mk 14:22), may suggest the goal of every Christian's journey as he receives (takes) the body of Christ in the eucharist. Certainly John uses *soma* with a symbolic meaning in 2:21. Interestingly a 14th century writer, Ludolphus de Saxonia, draws a homiletic analogy between Nicodemus' action and communicants at the eucharist – "the faithful who share in the body of Christ from the altar (*de altari*) are equivalent to those who took him down from the cross (*de cruce*)" (*Vita Iesu Christi* pars II:65:4).

Whether John intended this or not, the Passion Narrative as a whole recalls to Christians the death of Christ as the central element of their faith which they set forth in the eucharist. They do this not as though the cross is simply a matter of past history, but as bearing witness to the living Lord of the church whose body, or person, they receive in the eucharist. In so doing they not only proclaim the Lord's death until he should come, but they also recognize their own participation in his death as the way in which they can share in his life.

John has indicated in various ways throughout his gospel that the passion of Jesus is the fulfilment of scripture. Far from being a disastrous tragedy, it was a glorious display of the triumph of God. Here in the cross light overcomes darkness. Explicit references to this as the fulfilment of scripture occur for the first time in 12:38, but the theme has been there all along and is now disclosed at the cross. So because Jesus is the light of the world (8:12; cf Is 60:1) John, unlike the synoptics, has no record of darkness at the crucifixion. All that happens to Jesus is in accordance with scripture. Not only are there the allusions to the servant of God of Isaiah, as already noted, but the details of the Passion are to be seen as foreshadowed in the Old Testament. So John refers to Psalm 22 and Psalm 69, psalms which were already in use in Christian worship with reference to the Passion, as is shown by the use made by all four evangelists, either in quotation or by allusion, and by their use by other writers of the New Testament (as in 1 Pet 5:8 and Rom 11:9-10). This theme of fulfilment is specially strong in John 19:28, where John uses the word *teleiothe* (completed, accomplished) instead of the more usual word meaning "fulfilled" (*plerothe* – 19:24). The change of verb appears to be deliberate to show that both scripture and his own mission (*tetelestai* – it is accomplished 19:30) find their fulfilment on the cross (cf Amsler 1960:39,n2).

If, as seems likely, the Passion Narrative had its original *Sitz im Leben* in the celebration at Passover by Jewish Christians of the death of Christ, its relation in general outline to the eucharist is not difficult to see. For the eucharist itself is the *anamnesis* of Christ's death and resurrection, and though later on the Passion Narrative would have been read on many occasions, its meaning would be specially apparent in a eucharistic context. The eucharist is specially concerned with the three themes of the Passion Narrative which have been noted – the person and work of Christ, the unity between the disciples and their Lord, and the cross of Christ as the culmination of all God's purposes found in the Old Testament. So the acts of Christian worship, especially baptism and eucharist, reflect the two aspects of the gospel – the declaration of God's love in Christ and the challenge to the disciple to respond in faith and to share in the Lord's cross and risen life.

8

Jesus, the sign of life

The most foundational sense in which stories are
part of Christianity is their routinized form in
Christian rituals.

S W Sykes The role of story in the Christian
religion: An hypothesis. *Literature and Theology 1*
(1987) 25

Resurrection and life

"In him was life, and the life was the light of men" (1:4). The
description of the Word as the source of life is applied
throughout the gospel in various ways to the historical person
of Jesus, who is thus shown truly to be the incarnate Word. So
he is "the bread of life" (6:35) and indeed life itself – "I am
resurrection and I am life (*he zoe*)" (11:25). When he affirms "I
am the way and the truth and life (*he zoe*)" (14:6), he is claiming
for himself the attributes which could be applied to the Torah
(Ps 1). In so doing he replaces the Torah as the giver of life. Life
is itself a symbol, and in the fourth gospel it is inextricably bound
up with the person of Jesus and the response which men and
women are called to make to him. To respond to him in obedience is to believe in him, and so find life (3:15-16). So life
means neither simply biological life, nor simply life in the future,
though both features are embraced by it. It refers especially to
the fullness of life which is to be found in the recognition of its

meaning, as revealed in the human life of Jesus, the incarnate Word of God.

This life is described as "life eternal" (*zoe aionios*) for the first time in John in 3:15. This was a term used in late Judaism (Dan 12:2; 4 Macc 15:3; Ps Sol 3:12) to refer to life after death in the age to come. There the epithet "eternal" (*aionios*) represented the adverbial phrase "for the age", "for ever" (*eis ton aiona*, e g Ps Sol 8:34; 11:7,9; 13:11; 14:31), which translates the common Hebrew expression *l⁽e⁾'olam* (e g 1 Kg 1:31). This Old Testament meaning of the phrase is regularly found in the synoptics (Mk 10:17 par; 10:30 par; Lk 10:25; Mt 25:46), where it probably reflects the language of Jesus as he speaks from his Jewish background. The phrase is also used by Paul (e g Rom 2:7; 5:21). The simple *zoe* (life) with the same meaning is found not only in John but also in the synoptics and Paul (Mk 9:43; Mt 18:8; Rom 7:10). Mark's reference to the kingdom of God in 9:45 is represented in the parallel passage in Matthew (18:9) by *zoe* (life), which is of interest in view of the way in which the only two references to the kingdom of God in John (3:3,5) are apparently synonymous with John's use of the phrase "life eternal". The use of the phrase in the New Testament reflects the general Jewish understanding of it as referring to the future, though there are signs of a development in its meaning to refer to the quality, rather than the permanence, of life.

The fourth gospel does not deny the understanding of life in the future (5:28-29; 6:58), but it now links it firmly with faith in the person of Jesus as providing not simply life for ever, but life in the present. In John 3:36, for example, present and future are brought closely together – "He who believes in the Son *has* eternal life: he who disobeys the Son *will not see* life, but the wrath of God abides on him".

For the fourth gospel, therefore, the concept of life cannot be dissociated from the person of Jesus, who is revealed by his signs, his *semeia*, of which the Passion may be regarded as the climax. Here in the humble and free submission to a shameful death, already anticipated in the foot-washing of chapter 13, he revealed the love of God for his own (13:1; 15:13). Here too he revealed the meaning of life, that it is only in fellowship with him in his obedience and his death that his disciples are to find life, what some would call "authentic being". The same idea is expressed by the synoptics (e g Mk 8:34-37), even though the phrase "eternal life" is not used. The gospels were written primarily for Christians to assure them of the offer of life made by Jesus the Lord, and to help them explore more deeply the meaning of this life. So the phrase "the light of life" (Jn 8:12) describes the meaning which Jesus gives to life, as is dramatically presented in chapter 9. The purpose of the incarnation is again similarly described in 10:10 – "I have come that they might have life, and have it in abundance" (cf 10:28). The life is given in Jesus through his revelation of the Father.

This revelation is especially declared on the cross: this is the moment of glorification. In the synoptic account the glorification is seen as taking place after and as a result of the cross, expressed clearly in Luke 24:26. The synoptics start with the historical, incarnate life of Jesus, leading to the cross, so that the uniqueness of his person is expressed by Matthew and Luke especially in the resurrection. John, on the other hand, adopts a different approach. He starts with the reference to the eternal Word of God, the *logos*, one with the Father, the source of life and the revealer of the Father. This eternal Word of God became a human being and dwelt among us. If Mark therefore tried to answer the question "Why did Jesus have to be crucified if he is really the Messiah?", John represents the crucifixion as the victorious culmination of the display of God's love. The resurrection, therefore, because of the person of Jesus, the *logos* incarnate, is a foregone conclusion. He who is one with God (1:1; 10:30) cannot be held in the power of death (cf Ac 2:24), however real his death was seen to be (19:34-35).

The resurrection narrative of the fourth gospel describes the different ways in which the followers of Jesus came to express their faith in him. The first pericope (20:1-10) describes the way in which the Beloved Disciple came to faith. Peter and he had run together to the sepulchre, and Peter went straight in and saw that the body had gone and that the burial wrappings were lying there. "So the other disciple too, who had reached the sepulchre first, went in and saw and believed" (20:8). The use of the word "so" (*oun* – therefore) is of special interest. Perhaps it implies that Peter told John (if we may accept the identification) what he had seen, and therefore John went in to investigate for himself. He saw the same as Peter, and yet he believed, he made his act of faith, whereas Peter apparently remained in doubt. Here is a good example of the ambiguity of signs in the fourth gospel. Peter and John saw the same thing: but only John believed. He did not need to see the risen Christ: the signs of Jesus' departure from the sepulchre were enough for him. In the narrative Mary of Magdala had already described Jesus as the Lord (*kurios*, 20:2), and John's act of faith was a recognition of his Lordship.

The next scene is rather different (20:11-18). Whereas Peter and John went back to the disciples, presumably because John at least knew that the Lord had risen, Mary stayed at the sepulchre in tears. She saw the risen Lord without realizing who he was (like the disciples in Luke's gospel on the way to Emmaus), until he addressed her by name. The Lord indeed has risen: but the acknowledgement of this is due not simply to observation or to the truth of history, but to the establishment of a relationship between the Lord and the disciple, and the acceptance of the relationship. So in recognition and in answer to Jesus' address she calls him "My rabbi (teacher)". Jesus' next words "Do not touch me" are ambiguous. The present imperative which is used there can have one of two meanings. It can mean either "Stop touching me" or "Do not hold on to me". The latter meaning would seem to be more likely, as there has been no intimation that Mary had in fact touched him. In this case the meaning would seem to be that disciples cannot ask for physical signs of Christ's bodily presence apart from his completed work marked by his ascension to the Father. So the next sentence implies that there will be a time when it will be possible to touch him, when signs of his presence will be given: "Do not hold me, *for* I have not yet ascended to the Father."

Here we have the last "not yet" of the gospel: the theme of looking forward to the completion of Jesus' work has been present from the beginning. It was clearly seen in John 2:4 – "My hour has not yet come" – but it can be detected too in 1:18 – "No-one has ever yet (*popote*) seen God". So the last "not yet" (*oupo*) of the gospel prepares the way for the final act of the drama, and implies that it will be possible to touch the risen Lord when he has ascended (cf Shaw 1974:20). The final sentence of verse 17 assures the disciples of the unity which they share with the risen Lord, as he joins them with himself: "I am ascending to my Father and to your Father and to my God and your God." The fellowship or unity between Jesus and the disciples, already anticipated in 15:1-8, 17:20-26 and 19:26-27, means that they will be the visible signs of Christ's presence in the world. But first Jesus must ascend to the Father. In the fourth gospel the ascension appears to be considered as taking place between the appearance to Mary and the appearance to the disciples, since in 20:27 Thomas is invited to touch the Lord. So the implication of the "not yet" is that after the ascension some form of touching will be possible. Marsh (1968:638) comments: "It is far from fancy to think that John may well be making clear to Christians that it is with the risen and ascended, the glorified Christ that they have communion, on whom they feed, in the eucharist." Shaw (1974:23) too believes that this verse is concerned with the reality of the presence of the ascended Christ with his people in the eucharist. "The problem in chapter 20 is 'How can we touch his body when he is not here?' ", and he believes that the answer is supplied by 6:62-63, where the reference to the ascension is followed by the words "It is the Spirit who gives life".

Although there may well be this eucharistic allusion in 20:17 it is far from clear by itself, and it would seem more likely that it serves as an introduction to the next episode, which is presented in two parts (20:19-23 and 20:24-29) which are closely linked together. Once again the central feature of this disclosure incident is the difficulty of recognizing the risen Lord. Thomas refused to believe the witness of the other disciples to whom the Lord appeared. Thomas, whose name is significantly translated into Greek, is the twin or symbol of every Christian who wants to recognize the Lord's presence. Both sections of the narrative are carefully constructed, the whole of which provides the climax of the resurrection account and of the gospel. In view therefore of the liturgical allusions throughout the gospel and of the eucharistic hint in 20:17, it would not be surprising to find in this climax a clear eucharistic reference. Such an expectation is amply confirmed by an examination of the passage.

The day of resurrection – the first day of every week: John 20:19-29

The first point to notice is the parallelism between several features in verses 19 to 23 and 24 to 29, which demonstrates the unity of the whole episode. We are dealing not with two incidents, but with one incident comprising two parts, each of which is necessary for the understanding of the whole. The parallel features in the two parts are as follows: the references to the physical marks of the crucifixion, in his hands and his side (vv20,25,27); the same day of the week (vv19,26); the greeting of peace (vv19,21,26); the joy of the disciples at seeing the Lord (v20) and Thomas' cry of worship (v28).

The repetition of these features in both parts of the narrative shows the importance which John attributed to them. They were deliberately used to convey his message, and they gain in significance when considered in a eucharistic context. The first day of the week, when the disciples were gathered together, has always been the special day of Christian worship, especially for the eucharist, since the first day of the week is the day of resurrection, otherwise known as the third day (i e after the crucifixion; cf 2:1). The doors were shut: the earliest eucharistic liturgies show the importance of ensuring that only the faithful (*hoi pistoi*) are present and that all non-Christians (*hoi apistoi*) are excluded. So the so-called Clementine liturgy of the third or fourth century contains the cry of the deacon: "Let no-one who is unqualified draw near: as many of us as are faithful (*pistoi*), let us bend the knee" (Brightman 1896:9). Though this is evidence of a much later date, a similar rule is prescribed by Didache 10:6, and seems to be suggested by 2 Corinthians 6:15 – "What agreement is there between Christ and Beliar? Or what share has a Christian (*pistos*) with a non-Christian (*apistos*)?". In the fourth gospel the Jews are usually presented as the type of non-believers, those who have not put their faith in Jesus Christ, by making their act of commitment in baptism. The reference to the Jews in verse 19, therefore, may be due not to fear of attack by them, but to fear of having unbelievers in the eucharistic gathering. In the Liturgy of St James the deacon cries at the Great Entrance before the Peace "No catechumen; no uninitiated; no-one unable to be joined with us. Take note of each other. The doors." (Brightman 1896:41). The closing of the doors in John 20:19 may well represent a primitive custom later elaborated in the liturgies.

"The disciples" (*mathetai*) is as much a description of the later as of the first followers of Jesus: John's regular use of *mathetai*, and never of *apostoloi* (apostles), to describe the twelve may be due to his desire to help later disciples see that they are as surely in the presence of Jesus as the original twelve were. When the disciples were together on the first day of the week, with the faithless Jews excluded, Jesus came and stood in their midst. Many commentators seem to miss the point here in thinking that the risen Jesus' ability to pass through closed doors is due to his divine nature (Loisy 1921:505; Bultmann 1971:691; Barrett 1978:567; Haenchen 1984b:210), and that this is what John wishes to represent. In fact there is no real mystery, and no need to describe the manner of Jesus' appearing. Where the church is gathered in Christ's name, there he is in their midst (cf Mt 18:20; 28:20) as Lindars (1972:610) recognizes. The presence of the Lord with his disciples in every age is as real as it was with the first disciples on the first Easter. This is especially true when the church meets to make eucharist. The later tendency to try to define a moment of consecration to mark, as it were, the coming of Christ in the eucharist obscures the earlier and more scriptural understanding of his presence. He is present with and in his people when they make *anamnesis* of the event by which they were constituted his people. This explains too why there is no reference in these verses to Jesus' departure: he did not depart, for he who makes himself present to his disciples is in them and with them. Similarly, at the end of every eucharist the Lord does not depart, but goes with the worshippers in their lives.

The address "Peace to you" is no mere formal greeting: its repetition shows the importance which John assigns to it, and its recurrence in the meeting with Thomas emphasizes it still more. The greeting presumably refers back to 14:27. It is therefore no ordinary greeting: "Peace I leave with you, my peace I give to you: not as the world gives it do I give it to you." Peace (*šalôm*) describes the restored relationship between God and human beings which has been effected by the death and resurrection of Jesus Christ. By the reference back to 14:27, with its anticipation of Jesus' death and return to the Father (14:28-31), the giving of the Peace is linked to the Passion. In the earliest liturgies (Justin *Apol* 1:65) the kiss of peace was symbolically given as a sign that what follows is a way of entering into, and making present the peace won through Christ, and at the same time a sign of the unity and fellowship of Christians with each other in Christ as they meet to give thanks for the peace which they enjoy in him. In the liturgy of St James, for example, the greeting "Peace to all" occurs frequently, and especially before the offertory (Brightman 1896:49). The injunction of Paul "Greet one another with a holy kiss" (Rom 16:16; 1 Cor 16:20; 2 Cor 13:12) is frequently found in the early liturgies at this point. Though the liturgies are to be dated to the third or fourth centuries, the presence of this injunction in the letters of Paul, as well as in 1 Peter 5:14, witnesses to an early liturgical practice, apparently especially connected to the eucharist, as 1 Corinthians 16:22-23 (with the liturgical phrases "let him be anathema"; *"Marana tha"*; "the grace of the Lord Jesus") suggests. The importance of the Peace is shown by the way in which it has survived through the centuries and has been restored to many modern rites.

On the first Easter day Jesus showed his disciples his hands and his side, the marks of his wounds. At every eucharist, from the earliest times, the risen Lord assured his disciples of his presence by the signs of his body and his blood, which refer back to his death and resurrection of which the eucharist is the *anamnesis*. As the first disciples recognized their crucified and risen Lord by the outward evidence, so at every eucharist the disciples are given the opportunity to do the same. The disciples were glad (*echaresan* – v20) when they saw the Lord : they shared in the joy (*chara*) which no-one would take from them (16:22).

The peace which the risen Christ brings to his disciples involves them in mission. Those who know his peace and the joy which it brings cannot keep it to themselves. The peace of Christ, like his body, his own self, is given to be shared. As Jesus Christ has been sent by the Father, so he sends his disciples: he is with them and in them: where they go he goes too. Westcott (1908:298) draws attention to the significance of the perfect tense (*apestalken* – has sent) as indicating that the mission of Christ himself is now carried on in and through the disciples, who act not with their own authority, but as envoys of Christ.

The risen Christ breathes on them (v22), that is, he gives them the Holy Spirit, his Spirit. By the use of the word *enephusesen* (breathed into), which occurs only here in the New Testament, John reflects its use in Genesis 2:7, and so portrays this event as the re-enactment of God's gift of life to Adam. Here is a new creation by the new Adam. The words accompanying the gift – "Receive Holy Spirit" – may recall Mark 14:22 and refer to the narrative of the institution of the eucharist. This however should not be pressed. The word for "receive" (*labete*) is the same in John as in Mark, but it is a very common word, and is regularly used for the reception of the Spirit (e g Ac 8:15; 19:2). It is nevertheless important to recognize the part which John assigns to the Spirit in the mystery of salvation. The action of the Holy Spirit is essentially connected with, and arises from, the glorification of Christ upon the cross (see especially 7:39). In drawing special attention in 20:22 to the Spirit John wishes to show the intimate connection between the coming of the Holy Spirit to the disciples and the death and resurrection of Jesus. John presents this connection in a way which helps his hearers or readers to see the action of the Spirit in every *anamnesis* of the Lord's death and resurrection.

Eastern liturgies emphasized the part of the Holy Spirit in the eucharist, especially in the consecration of the elements (Brightman 1896:21) so that the invocation (*epiklesis*) of the Holy Spirit is seen as the moment (if such is to be sought for) of consecration. There is no suggestion of this view in the New Testament. Dix (1945:398) notes that apparently in Cyril of Jerusalem (late fourth century) "a new idea, that of the 'transformation' or 'conversion' of the elements finds clear liturgical expression", whereas previously the Holy Spirit was invoked with reference to the benefits of communion and the blessing of the communicants. This earlier view seems to correspond very closely with John's view of the part of the Spirit in the work of salvation, which believers would know was made present in the eucharist.

The commission of verse 23 – "Whose soever sins you forgive, they *have been* forgiven; whose soever sins you retain, they *have been* retained" – is presumably to be regarded as given to the church as a whole, since all are equally disciples of Christ. The words were later connected with the sacrament of penance, but in all probability they originally referred to the general authority of the church (the local congregation) to forgive sins (Mt 18:18), and especially to admit believers into the church by baptism (Loisy 1921:508). Barrett (1985:73) expresses himself even more strongly: "Here we seem to be very near a command to baptize *eis aphesin hamartion*, 'for the forgiveness of sins'; but it is significant that even here, as in John 3 and 13, there is no explicit mention of the rite." John, it has been urged throughout the preceding chapters, does not need to make himself explicit. He is helping his readers or hearers to discover as though by themselves the allusion which he makes. This is John's way of describing the baptismal commission of Matthew 28:19-20. It is particularly apt for the fourth gospel in view of the Baptist's witness in 1:29 "There is the Lamb of God who takes away the sin of the world". Words spoken in the context of baptism allude too to the offering of the Lamb of God on the cross. But John 20:23 is very appropriate in a eucharistic context, since it reminds believers that every meeting with the risen Christ in the eucharist is also a summons to mission and service.

These considerations lead us to take very seriously the view that John was deliberately writing his account of the resurrection against the background of the church's worship of the late first century, centred around the eucharist. This is not to deny the historical reality of the resurrection, but to view it as an event which, though rooted in history, transcends history. In other words, the resurrection is as real for believers of today as it was for the disciples at the first Easter.

John 20:24-29

Such a view of verses 19 to 23 is supported by examining verses 24 to 29 in a similar way. It has already been noted (p 150) that several features of the account of the earlier appearance have been deliberately repeated in verses 24 to 29. Not only is there the repetition of the greeting "Peace be with you", but once again it is on the first day of the week, when the doors have been shut, that the risen Christ meets with the disciples. Again he shows them the signs of his wounds. The account of the appearance to Thomas has been given in order to drive home the meaning not only of 20:19-23 but also of 20:1-18. There was no reason why Thomas' absence at the first appearance of the Lord should be mentioned. The story is told to emphasize the reality of the Lord's presence with disciples of every age who, like Thomas, when presented with the signs of his passion responded in adoration. Hoskyns (1947:549) notes that "The narrative (*sc* of chapter 20) is ... a carefully constructed literary whole". The structure of the pericope shows clearly that it must be closely taken with the rest of the chapter. Further, the chapter is really the conclusion of the gospel and as such has much to say about the meaning of the gospel as a whole. This does not mean that chapter 21 is to be disregarded, since it is an integral part of the gospel as we have it. But however one regards it, 20:30-31 is at least *an* ending, if not *the* ending, of the gospel. Chapter 21 can well be considered to be an epilogue confirming, if not explaining, what has gone before.

Cullmann (1953:43) believes that the Thomas story "holds, as it were, the Johannine understanding of the whole life of Jesus". The narrative (vv24-29) however must not be dissociated from what precedes it: it is the Thomas story in its connection with verses 1 to 23 that provides the clue to John's understanding not only of the life of Jesus, but of the Christian response to it. The resurrection is the vindication of the person of the incarnate Word of God, and the assurance of his presence through the Holy Spirit with his disciples in every age.

The leading idea of verses 24 to 29 is that Thomas refuses to believe without satisfactory visible evidence. Thomas the twin, a type of Christian disciples, may be contrasted with the Beloved

Disciple who saw the empty tomb and believed (v8). He saw nothing but made his act of faith. Thomas on the other hand wanted firm evidence, which is supplied at a further meeting of the disciples. Jesus appears to them, because once again they are met in his name, and he invites Thomas to touch him, to thrust his hand into his side. The contrast between this and the words spoken to Mary Magdalene is clearly deliberate. What then has happened in the narrative to make it possible for Thomas to touch the risen Jesus? Dodd is surely right in suggesting (1954:442-443) that the event which marks the fulfilment of Jesus' mission is his risen appearance to the disciples and his gift to them of the Spirit. John, as is widely recognized, telescopes the events of resurrection, ascension and the giving of the Spirit into a single day, thereby connecting the whole Christ-event with the Passion. Jesus' presence with the disciples in the Spirit is firmly assured, and it is this which is signified and made real at every eucharist.

Verses 26 to 29 are set in the same eucharistic context as verses 19 to 23. Later disciples, as unbelieving as Thomas, are offered signs in the eucharist as sure as those offered to Thomas. Like Thomas therefore they are to be no longer unbelieving (*apistos*), but believing (*pistos*), enrolled among the faithful. The response which is required is the response made by Thomas, acknowledging the risen Christ as "My Lord and my God". Verse 29a is presumably a question – "Is it because you have seen me that you have believed?" – and a contrast is drawn between those like Thomas who need to see signs, and those like the Beloved Disciple who can come to faith without the need of the same visible evidence (v8). In the eucharist signs are provided which point to the reality of Christ's resurrection: but such signs need the attitude of faith and commitment if their meaning is to be appreciated, and therefore they too need to be seen as pointing to the Lordship of Christ.

Thüsing believes that there is no explicit reference to the eucharist intended in these verses, which are meant to confirm the reality which forms the foundation of the sacraments. "That the believers have in the eucharist communion with the body of the Risen One is for the evangelist self-evident. Even though he did not express it he certainly did not wish it to be excluded"

(1970:282, translated). Barrett (1978:573) believes that verse 28 "may be liturgical in origin". Brown too suggests (1970:1019) some kind of liturgical setting. It is certainly in line with the method of writing which John seems to have been following. John was telling the story of the resurrection in ways which could remind believers that what they were doing in their worship was in fact the proclamation of the gospel and their response to it. Very likely the exclamation of Thomas had its counterpart in the liturgy of John's day (cf 1 Cor 12:3), but as Thüsing rightly observes John is primarily concerned not with the eucharist but with the story of Jesus' resurrection, which is the foundation of every eucharistic celebration. The readers or hearers of the gospel are to make the connection for themselves. This seems to be the way in which Loisy understood the incident: in commenting on the words "Peace to you" of 20:26, he says that the editor of the gospel has deliberately repeated the phrase from 20:19,21 "to emphasize the typical meaning of the meeting, similar to those of the first Christian communities in their eucharistic assemblies" (1921:510, translated).

In 20:29 the question is raised for believers of John's day: "How can we who have not seen Jesus believe in the Lord?" It was a question which confronted Paul, to which he responded "Our conduct is determined by faith, not by sight" (2 Cor 5:7 – *dia pisteos ... ou dia eidous*). Similarly 1 Peter 1:8, in what seems to be a baptismal context talks of Jesus Christ "whom you love though you have not seen (*idontes*, aorist) him, on whom you believe even though you do not see (*horontes*, present) him now, and so you rejoice with an unspeakable joy ...". The need of faith is expressed by all three writers. The context in which John described the resurrection helps people understand that though they do not see Jesus they do have signs of his presence with them in their worship.

John 20 and 1:1-18

Since chapter 20 may be considered to be the final chapter of the gospel, it is instructive to compare it with chapter 1 so that its significance may be clarified both as the conclusion of the gospel and as a clue to the understanding of the eucharist. The Prologue begins with the utterance of God's word in a unique way in Jesus, in order that all might come to faith (1:7, where the aorist *pisteusosin* is to be noted) and find life. 1:6 refers to the witness of a man named John, whose real work was to bear witness to Jesus as the source of life and light (1:4,7,8). Though the primary reference is to John the Baptist, it is possible to see here a hidden reference to the evangelist too, who otherwise remains anonymous. Certainly the evangelist's purpose is the same as that of the Baptist, to help people believe in Christ and so find life (cf Barth 1986:52). The last two verses of chapter 20 therefore sum up the purpose of the gospel already adumbrated in 1:7.

In 1:12, to those who received (*elabon*) the *logos* "he gave the right to become children of God, to those who believe in his name" – an idea which would without much difficulty remind Christians of their baptism. In 20:22 the risen Christ bids the disciples "Receive (*labete*) Holy Spirit": in receiving the Spirit, they are receiving Christ and putting their faith in him. Here are his own (*hoi idioi*, 1:11) really showing themselves to be his own, the faithful, unlike the disbelieving Jews, who were "his own" to whom the Word came, and who did not receive him but handed him over to Pilate (18:30). They would receive him especially in their baptism and in eucharist. "The Word became flesh and made his dwelling among us, and we beheld his glory" (1:14): these words provide a summary of one aspect of the incarnation. The display of God's glory is seen in Jesus Christ, in his obedience and utter consecration to the will of his Father and in his love for men and women. These two features – Christ's obedience and his love for men and women – meet on the cross. The vindication of this human life of obedience and love is provided by the resurrection and the appearance of the risen Lord to his disciples. So Thomas recognizes the glory of God in the crucified and risen Christ, and exclaims "My Lord and my God", the only explicit reference to Christ as God outside the Prologue. In Thomas' cry the Word who is God (1:1) is identified with the crucified and risen Christ now present with his disciples. He who came to dwell among men and women is still among them, and God's glory is with them claiming recognition in the assembly of those who profess his name.

John 1:18 ("No-one has ever yet seen God") provides, as we have seen, the first rather hidden "not yet". It continues "the only one, God, (or perhaps more likely 'the only son') who is in the Father's bosom, has made him known". The final Greek word of the sentence (*exegesato*) is in the aorist tense, and so indicates that the disclosure of God is made known as a completed action, by what Jesus did rather than simply by his person. The rest of the gospel is an account of this disclosure. Throughout the gospel there is the reference to the coming of Jesus' hour which is reached on the cross. But even then Mary may not touch Jesus, for he has not yet come to the disciples and given them the Spirit. Only after the giving of the Spirit is Thomas invited to touch, and only then does he express his faith – "My Lord and my God". God, "whom no-one has ever yet seen" (1:18) has indeed been disclosed in Christ.

The eucharistic allusions of chapter 20 are not meant to promote the eucharist as such, but rather to show that the eucharist celebrated by the church is no mere liturgical rite, but the setting forth of God's glory and the revelation of his gracious work in Christ. It offers to worshippers the visible signs of Christ's presence and redemptive love, and calls forth from them their continued faith in Christ their Lord and God. In the eucharistic gathering God's presence with his people is assured, and Christians are brought to see once more that they participate in the new age as surely as the first disciples who greeted their risen Lord. The evidence for the resurrection is to be found not simply or primarily as a fact of past history experienced by the first disciples, but in Christ's abiding presence with his church which, as it makes eucharist, sets forth the grounds of its faith and is caught up into heaven with the people of God. John's dramatic artistry, evident throughout the gospel, reaches its climax in chapter 20.

The final appearance: John 21

After chapter 20 any addition would seem to be rather an anti-climax. There is however no evidence that the fourth gospel ever circulated without chapter 21, so that its significance may not be neglected. Certainly the author responsible for the final form of the gospel was careful to integrate the chapter into the rest of the narrative. The theme of the disclosure of the glory of God in Jesus runs throughout the gospel. The first use of the word meaning "to manifest" or "to reveal" (*phaneroun*) describes the task of the Baptist that Jesus "might be revealed to Israel" (1:31). It is used again after the sign at Cana by which "Jesus manifested (or revealed) his glory" (2:11), and occurs throughout the gospel, so that in 17:6 Jesus exclaims "I revealed your name to those whom you gave me out of the world". So now in chapter 21 he manifests himself to those who believed in him (vv1 *bis*,14).

Among the five disciples who are identified by name are the two sons of Zebedee, to provide a clue to the name of the Beloved Disciple (21:2). This would be in line with the suggestion that 1:6 contains an allusion to the evangelist, and both would accord with the general allusive style of writing found in the fourth gospel. Thomas the twin, as he has been earlier called in the gospel, the specially symbolic disciple, is there, and so too is Nathanael, whose connection with Cana is noted and who now sees the greater things which he was promised in 1:51, of which a preview was given at Cana. The disciples are at the sea of Tiberias, mentioned again in John only at 6:1,23, on whose shore the feeding of the five thousand took place, in the account of which the Johannine word for fish (*opsarion*) was used (6:9,11), as it is also used in 21:9,10,13.

There is therefore plenty of evidence to show that the author of chapter 21 was familiar with the method and style adopted throughout the gospel, and though Shaw (1975) is right to note the difference of emphasis in the imagery of the chapter, the chapter nevertheless shows a real understanding of the drift of the argument of the rest of the gospel. So the way in which the meal by the sea is set in a context which reflects both that of Cana and that of the miraculous feeding helps to show the eucharistic allusions not only of chapter 21 but also of 2:1-11 and of chapter 6.

Chapter 21 appears to combine two different and originally

independent traditions. The first is the fishing expedition and the miraculous catch, which has obvious affinities with Luke 5:1-11, and which is concerned with the mission of the church to all nations, the Gentiles. For the enigmatic number 153 refers at least to the universal scope of the mission, which, if it is to succeed, must be carried out in obedience to the Lord. The promise of Jesus in Mark 1:17 – "Follow me and I will make you fishers of men" – is transposed in the fourth gospel until after the resurrection, for it was then that the disciples were commissioned and sent to carry on the mission of Christ (20:21).

The second originally independent story concerns the meal on the shore. There is no clear connection between the two, for in spite of the wonderful catch it is Jesus who provides the bread and the fish (v9). He does so at a fire (*anthrakia*, used only at 18:18 and 21:9). It was by a fire that Peter had stood trying to warm himself at the time of trial. Now as the result of meeting the Lord around another fire he is given the chance to rehabilitate himself, as his three-fold protestation of love (21:15-17) shows his repentance for his three-fold denial. The story of the meal resembles the recognition scene at the breaking of the bread in Luke 24:30-31, but in a much less obvious manner. Although apparently the disciples knew that he was the Lord, they did not dare ask him (v12). It is only after the meal that verse 14 records that Jesus was revealed to the disciples for the third time after he had risen.

The two traditions have been combined to produce what Shaw (1974:18) has called "a profound yet practical missionary assertion that the apostolic work of the Church is to gather all men into Christ in his eucharist". In a gospel through which eucharistic and baptismal allusions run like a thread this story forms a fitting conclusion.

The chapter ends with the moving predictions of the destinies of two of the missionaries or apostles, Peter and John, reminding the readers that in Christ past failure is no bar to future success, and that disciples are called to carry out their missionary task in different ways. It may be that the gospel ends not with a bang but a whimper, in view of the climax reached in 20:28 with the confession of faith of Thomas the twin. But chapter 21 is the assertion that the Lord who died on the cross is still in control and continues his work through his disciples, to whom he gives life in abundance as they feed on him, the bread of life. Through them Christ carries on his work of reconciliation, and he meets with them in their worship where they recall his death and resurrection which is for them the sign of life.

Epilogue

The meaning of life for the Christian today

Every New Testament text ... is simultaneously
speaking to the tradition and to the needs of new
audiences who must integrate its message into their
situation but also their situation into its world.

J M Reese *Experiencing the Good News* (Glazier
1984) 186

The previous chapters have had one aim, to consider the thesis
that the fourth gospel reflects the worship of the early church,
and therefore makes frequent allusions to it which would have
been recognized by those for whom it was written. In this way
people were to be helped to realize not only that the promises
of the Old Testament had been fulfilled, and the nature of
YHWH revealed, in Jesus Christ, but that Christ was now present as the risen Lord with his church. They were to find him in
every aspect of their life together, but they would express their
faith in him especially in the eucharist which he had entrusted
to them as his *anamnesis*. Even if it could be conclusively shown
that John was not at all concerned with baptism or eucharist in
composing his gospel, such a way of reading it would not be
inappropriate, since both the gospel and the acts of Christian
worship stem from the same event of God's revelation in Jesus
Christ, and both bear witness to it. Christians today can therefore be helped to find in many of the narratives and discourses

relationship between scripture and their acts of worship, and the significance of both for their life in the world.

Furthermore, if we take the gospel as a whole in the form in which it has been received into the canon, then eucharistic and baptismal references at any rate in some places seem inevitable. In fact, the so-called ecclesiastical redactions would seem to show that some early readers of the gospel recognized the allusions and wished to make them plain. De la Potterie, for example, it will be recalled, suggested (1962:440) that the words "water and" (*hudatos kai* – Jn 3:5) were added to the evangelist's source to make the reference to baptism beyond all doubt. Yet it is also clear, as Borgen demonstrates (1965:86-97) that one of the most significant eucharistic passages (Jn 6:51-58) is entirely in the style of the rest of the gospel. Although therefore it seems that the gospel went through several recensions before it reached its present form, all of them would seem to have arisen from the same community, presumably reflecting a shared understanding of the evangelist's meaning.

It will be remembered that Venetz (1976:111) stated that any congregation accustomed to celebrating baptism or eucharist could not fail to connect the words of John 19:34 with its acts of worship, and to discover in them the source of its faith and life, in so far as both baptism and eucharist took their meaning from the death of Christ. As he went on to recognize the legitimacy of such an interpretation, the question is raised "Where does meaning reside?". Does the meaning of a text depend on discovering the meaning which the author intended? Certainly the discovery of the author's intended meaning – if we can ever be sure of it – helps to locate the text in a historical context, just as knowledge of the historical context helps us to arrive at the author's meaning. But the meaning of a literary text is by no means exhausted when we have discovered what the author actually meant.

Any great literary text – a description which certainly applies to the bible – has the power to challenge its readers in ways which its author may never have contemplated. It is this feature which gives to the text the possibility of diverse meanings (cf Nineham 1978:267). As a consequence the meaning of a literary text can never be definitively analyzed or fully exhausted. The meaning of a literary text, as opposed, for example, to a legal text, lies not simply in the words themselves, but in the relationship established between the reader and the text. This is particularly true of a religious text which serves to confirm or to challenge the beliefs, attitudes and practices of the community whose text it is. The text indeed provides parameters to prevent bizarre interpretations, but each reader gives meaning to the text by the response made to it. So the comments of Malatesta (1977:177), already quoted, can profitably be repeated:

> ... the only adequate way for a Christian to "read" the text of John – or of any biblical text – is to see it *both* in its historical-critical sense *and* in the sense given by the theology and contemplation of Tradition, the liturgical prayer of the Church ... and the resonance of the text in the life of the people of God at any given period.

It is the last feature with which we are now concerned – "the resonance of the text in the life of the people of God at any given period". This is in fact how the bible has been interpreted throughout the centuries in different cultures. The iconography of the eastern church provides but one example. There the figure of Christ the Pantokrator ("he who rules over all") is frequently connected both with Old Testament figures and incidents (especially Abraham, Sarah and Melchizedek), and with the gospel narratives, which find their meaning in the liturgy of the church. A particularly striking example from the 14th century is in Kariye Camii, Istanbul – now a museum, formerly a mosque and originally a Christian church. Above the entrance to the inner narthex is a mosaic of Christ the Pantokrator, with the inscription "Jesus Christ the country of the living" (*Iesous Christos he chora ton zonton*). He holds the scriptures in his left hand and his right hand is raised in blessing. The panels immediately above depict the miracle at Cana (Jn 2:1-11) and the miraculous feeding (Jn 6). The mosaic is at the entrance to the church because it is in the liturgy that the worshippers find the meaning and fulfilment of scripture and share in the life of Christ through their participation in the eucharist. The church is the way into life: there one meets with Christ, the true source of life.

This kind of symbolism has been a mark of the eastern church from the earliest times, and demonstrates the way in which the gospels – especially the fourth gospel – were interpreted with reference to the liturgy. This liturgical background has been generally forgotten by Christians today, who tend to interpret the scriptures out of the context of their own experience. So we find Liberation theology in South America and Black theology and Liberation theology in South Africa. The text comes alive to the readers as they understand it as speaking to them in their own situation, so that they can identify not only with the people of the Exodus but with the poor and oppressed to whom Jesus offered deliverance (Lk 4:18). Such a contextualized approach has a real danger of limiting the universality of the gospel. In what respect can there be a valid way of reading the bible for blacks which does not apply to whites too? Such contextualization may often appear to be an attempt to domesticate the bible, so that what professes to be openness to fresh interpretative insights may in time well become the *only* method of interpretation, and then it ceases to be open. The final words of a book on the poetics of the bible (Prickett 1988:242) refer to "a conflict between open and closed systems of hermeneutics: those which claim to possess the Word, and those which are capable of being translated by it".

The signs – words and narratives – used in the scriptures are what constitute poetry, in the widest sense of the term, not of course in the sense that they are untrue, but because they enable believers to receive the word not simply as though it were something fixed and given, but rather as an opportunity to participate in it, to become creative (*poiesis* – creation) in giving it meaning for themselves and for others so as to be changed and transformed by it (cf Prickett 1988:45). The consequences of such a view could indeed be that the text is made to mean what the believer wants it to mean.

Some kind of control is therefore necessary so as to avoid extravagant interpretation. This control is really furnished by the life and faith of the church, especially as expressed in its liturgical worship which reflects its faith. So the well-known allegorical interpretation of the parable of the good Samaritan (Lk 10:30-37) by Augustine and others (which held sway for so many centuries) gave to the story a meaning which most commentators would agree was not what the author intended. In this interpretation the traveller symbolizes humanity on its journey to mortality (represented by Jericho, understood as similar to a word describing the waning moon). The wounded traveller symbolizes humanity overcome by sins. The man is left half-dead, unable to help himself and unable to be helped by Jewish rites, symbolized by the priest and Levite. The Samaritan (similar to a word meaning "guardian") stands for Christ, who lifts him up and takes him to the inn which is the church, whose inn-keeper is Paul, the two coins representing the two sacraments of the church. However far such an interpretation is both from the mind of Luke and from Jesus himself, at least it is controlled by the church's understanding of the person and work of Christ.

The New Testament scriptures arose from the context of the Christian community, involving a shared faith and background, and as time went on these same scriptures continued to form and shape the community and its life. It has sometimes been thought that the Johannine community was some kind of sectarian group away from the main stream of the church. But however unusual it may have been, there is no reason to doubt that it had a knowledge of the story of Jesus and of the customs and practices of the Christian community. If Bardesanes, whose orthodoxy has often been doubted, could in the second century contrast (according to MacMullen 1967:222) the ethical chaos prevailing in the Roman Empire with the life-style of Christians, saying "no matter where they live, no matter by what strange or wicked customs surrounded, Christians everywhere obey the same code", it would not be unreasonable to conclude that all Christians would be familiar with those rites by which they celebrated their redemption.

The view which has been urged in the previous chapters is that there is a consistent pattern throughout the fourth gospel whereby the text "resonates" with the liturgical acts by which worshippers are given life and meaning for their work in the world. This is not simply a matter for biblical scholars. It ought to be of profound significance for the church today, as it recognizes that the liturgy expresses in dramatic form the meaning of scripture and impels the church to see itself as sharing in the mission of Christ to bring his love and reconciliation to all people. The connection between liturgy and life was well expressed by a former prime minister of South Africa, DF Malan. In about 1949, in answer to a question about joint worship at the eucharist of blacks with whites, he said that if he were to share communion with blacks he would have to be ready to ask them to breakfast. Though apparently he was not ready to do this, at least he was right to see the connection between liturgy and life. What is expressed in the liturgy is to be expressed in daily life.

In the South African situation Christians have frequently been disobedient to the gospel in giving active or passive support to the policy of *apartheid* which separated people into different racial categories. Those churches, however, in which the eucharist has been the central act of worship have continually been challenged by their worship to recognize the fundamental fellowship (*koinonia*) which they have with each other in Christ, and to regard this as the expression of the unity which God wills for all whom he has created in his image. For the eucharist does not represent merely the unity of those actually present at any particular celebration: all eucharists are one eucharist, expressing the unity of all participants in Christ, however separated they may be from each other in time or place. All participants are branches of the one vine which is Christ. In the darkest days of *apartheid* there was no more telling witness to the unity which the Lord wills for all people than the joyful celebration of the eucharist in a multi-racial congregation expressing in various languages the praise of the Lord. Reading the fourth gospel in such a context brings out in a vivid way the meaning for today of such chapters as 15 and 17.

Just as the risen Christ sent out the disciples to carry on his mission in the world, so Christians are commissioned and empowered by the Spirit in baptism and eucharist to bear witness to the Lord in their personal, social and political life. Baptism is, as it was for John, the mark of the new start in life in fellowship with Christ and other Christians. The eucharist is the constant reaffirmation of the faithfulness of God and of the faith and commitment of the disciple, while both baptism and eucharist provide the assurance that the goal of God's purposes will be achieved – "I, if I be lifted up from the earth, will draw all people to me" (Jn 12:32). "The action of Jesus in the sacraments", says Thüsing, "is part of his 'drawing', by which he binds his own to his cross" (1970:174, translated).

The Christian church therefore is called to be a witness and a sign of God's purposes for the whole world. The fourth gospel urges disciples to bear witness to Christ, the sign of life, by whose suffering and service of love they have themselves been given life so that individually and corporately they too may be the sign of life in the world.

Works cited

Abbott, E A   1906.   *Johannine grammar.* London: Black.

Abbott, W M & Gallagher, J (eds)   1966.   *The documents of Vatican II.* London: Chapman.

Alter, R   [1987] 1989.   Introduction to the Old Testament, in Alter R & Kermode F (eds) *The literary guide to the Bible*, 11-35. Paperback. London: Fontana.

Amsler, S   1960.   *L'Ancien Testament dans l' église: Essai d'herméneutique chrétienne.* Neuchâtel: Delachaux & Niestlé.

Ashby, G W   1988.   *Sacrifice: its nature and purpose.* London: SCM.

Audet, J-P   1958.   *La Didachè :Instructions des apôtres.* Paris: Gabalda.

Aune, D E   1972.   *The cultic setting of realized eschatology in early Christianity.* Leiden: Brill (NovT Suppl 28).

Barrett, C K   1950.   The Holy Spirit in the fourth gospel. *JThS* ns 1, 8-15.

Barrett, C K   1978.   *The gospel according to St John: An introduction with commentary and notes on the Greek text.* 2nd edition. London: SPCK.

Barrett, C K   1985.   *Church, ministry and sacraments in the New Testament.* Exeter: Paternoster (The 1983 Didsbury Lectures).

Barth, K   1969.   *Church Dogmatics IV/4 (Fragment). The Christian life: Baptism as the foundation of the Christian life.* Edinburgh: T & T Clark.

Barth, K   1986.   *Witness to the word: A commentary on John 1.* Grand Rapids: Eerdmans.

Beckwith, R T   1978.   The Jewish background to Christian worship, in Jones, C, Wainwright, G & Yarnold, E (eds), *The Study of liturgy* 39-51. London: SPCK.

Blass, F & Debrunner, A   1961.   *A Greek grammar of the New Testament and other early Christian literature.* Translated and revised by R W Funk. Chicago: Chicago University Press.

Boismard, M-E   1956.   *Du baptême à Cana : Jean 1:19-2:11.* Paris:Cerf.

Boismard, M-E   1964.   Le lavement des pieds. *RB* 71, 5-24.

Borgen, P   1965.   *Bread from heaven: An exegetical study of the concept of manna in the gospel of John and the writings of Philo.* Leiden: Brill.

Borig, R   1967.   *Der wahre Weinstock:Untersuchungen zu Jo 15, 1-10.* Munchen: Kosel (SANT 16).

Bouyer, L 1966. *Eucharistie: Théologie et spiritualité de la prière eucharistique.* Tournai: Desclée.

Braun, F-M 1970. L'eucharistie selon saint Jean. *Rev Thomiste* 70, 5-29.

Brightman, F E (ed) 1896. *Liturgies Eastern and Western.* Oxford: Clarendon.

Brooks, O S 1963. The Johannine eucharist. *JBL* 82, 293-300.

Brown, R E 1965. *New Testament essays.* New York: Paulist Press.

Brown, R E 1966. *The gospel according to John (i-xii).* Garden City: Doubleday (Anchor Bible).

Brown, R E 1970. *The gospel according to John (xiii-xxi).* Garden City: Doubleday (Anchor Bible).

Brown, R E 1974. The relation of "The secret gospel of Mark" to the fourth gospel. *CBQ* 36, 466-485.

Brown, R E, Donfried, K P, Fitzmyer, J A & Reumann, J (eds) 1978. *Mary in the New Testament: A collaborative assessment by Protestant and Roman Catholic scholars.* London: Chapman.

Bultmann, R 1955a. *Essays philosophical and theological.* London: SCM.

Bultmann, R 1955b. *The theology of the New Testament II.* London: SCM.

Bultmann, R 1963. *The history of the synoptic tradition.* Oxford: Blackwell.

Bultmann, R 1971. *The gospel of John: A commentary.* Oxford: Blackwell.

Burge, G M 1987. *The anointed community: The Holy Spirit in the Johannine tradition.* Grand Rapids: Eerdmans.

Caird, G B 1980. *The language and imagery of the Bible.* London: Duckworth.

Chadwick, H 1967. *The early church.* Harmondsworth: Penguin (Pelican History of the Church).

Cohen, A P 1985. Symbolism and social change: matters of life and death in Whalsay, Shetland. *Man* ns 20, 307-324.

Corell, A 1958. *Consummatum est. Eschatology and church in the gospel of St. John.* London: SPCK.

Coutts, J 1957. Ephesians 1:3-14 and I Peter 1:3-12. *NTS* 3, 115-127.

Cullmann, O 1953. *Early Christian worship.* London: SCM (SBT 10).

Cullmann, O 1976. *The Johannine circle: Its place in Judaism, among the disciples of Jesus and in early Christianity. A study in the origin of the gospel of John.* London: SCM (N T Library).

Culpepper, A   1983.   *Anatomy of the fourth gospel: A study in literary design.* Philadelphia: Fortress.

Daly, R J   1978.   *Christian sacrifice: The Judaeo-christian background before Origen.* Washington: Catholic University of America (Studies in Christian antiquity).

Danby, H   1933.   *The Mishnah.* Oxford: Clarendon.

Daube, D   [1956] 1973.   *The New Testament and Rabbinic Judaism.* New York: Arno Press (Jordan lectures 1952).

De la Potterie, I   1962.   'Naître de l'eau et naître de l'Esprit': Le texte baptismal de Jn 3,5. *Sciences Ecclésiastiques* 14, 417-443.

Denis, A-M   1973.   Foi et exégèse. *NTS* 20, 45-54.

Derrett, J D M   1963.   Water into wine. *BZ* 7, 80-97.

Dix, G   1945.   *The shape of the liturgy.* 2nd ed. Westminster: Dacre.

Dix, G (ed)   1968.   *The treatise on the Apostolic Tradition of St Hippolytus of Rome.* Revised ed. Chadwick, H. London: SPCK.

Dodd, C H   1954.   *The interpretation of the fourth gospel.* Cambridge: Cambridge University Press.

Dodd, C H   1963.   *Historical tradition in the fourth gospel.* Cambridge: Cambridge University Press.

Donahue, J R   1976.   Introduction: From passion traditions to passion narrative, in Kelber, W H (ed), *The passion in Mark: Studies in Mark 14-16* 1-20. Philadelphia: Fortress.

Dunn, J D G   1971.   John VI – A eucharistic discourse? *NTS* 17, 328-338.

Dunn, J D G   1980.   *Christology in the making: A New Testament inquiry into the origins of the doctrine of the incarnation.* London: SCM.

Durkin, K   1987.   A eucharistic hymn in John 6? *ExpT* 98, 168-170.

Eliade, M   1979.   *A history of religious ideas.* Vol 1 *From the Stone Age to the Eleusinian Mysteries.* London: Collins.

Feuillet, A   1975.   *The priesthood of Christ and his ministers.* New York: Doubleday.

Feuillet, A   1985.   L'eucharistie, le sacrifice du Calvaire et le sacerdoce du Christ d'après quelques données du quatrieme évangile: comparaison avec les synoptiques et l'épître aux Hébreux. *Divinitas* 29 (2), 103-149.

Fortna, R T   1970.   *The gospel of signs.* Cambridge: Cambridge University Press (SNTSMS).

Gardner-Smith, P   1938.   *St John and the synoptic gospels.* Cambridge: Cambridge University Press.

Godet, F   1885.   *Commentary on the gospel of St John, with a critical introduction.* 3 vols. Edinburgh: T & T Clark.

Goodenough, E R   1956.   *Jewish symbols in the Greco-Roman period.* Vol 5: *Fish, bread and wine.* New York: Pantheon (BollS 37).

Goodenough, E R   1965.   *Jewish symbols in the Greco-Roman period.* Vol 12. New York: Pantheon (BollS 37).

Goppelt, L   1982.   *Theology of the New Testament.* vol 2. Grand Rapids: Eerdmans.

Goulder, M D   1982.   The liturgical origin of St John's gospel. *Stud Evang* 7, 205-221.

Greenslade, S L   1948.   *The church and the social order: A historical sketch.* London: SCM.

Grundmann, W   1959.   Das Wort von Jesu Freunden (Joh XV,13-16) und das Herrenmahl. *NovT* 3, 62-69.

Guilding, A   1960.   *The fourth gospel and Jewish worship.* Oxford: Oxford University Press.

Haenchen, E   1984a.   *John 1: A commentary on the gospel of John chapters 1-6.* Philadelphia:Fortress (Hermeneia).

Haenchen, E   1984b.   *John 2: A commentary on the gospel of John chapters 7-21.* Philadelphia: Fortress (Hermeneia).

Hanson, A T   1975.   *Grace and truth: A study in the doctrine of the incarnation.* London: SPCK.

Hanson, R P C   1960.   *God: Creator, saviour, spirit.* London: SCM.

Harkins, P W   1963.   *John Chrysostom: Baptismal instructions.* Westminster, Maryland: Newman Press (ACW 31).

Hengel, M   1989.   *The Johannine question.* London: SCM.

Hoskyns, E C   1947.   *The fourth gospel.* F N Davey (ed). 2nd ed. London: Faber.

Jeremias, J   1949.   *Die Wiederentdeckung von Bethesda.* Gottingen: Vandenhoef & Ruprecht.

Jeremias, J   1966.   *The eucharistic words of Jesus.* London: SCM.

Johnson, L T   1986.   *The writings of the New Testament.* Philadelphia: Fortress.

Jung, C G   1978.   Transformation symbolism in the Mass. *The Mysteries: Papers from the Eranos Yearbooks,* 274-336. Princeton: Princeton University Press (BollS 30.2).

Käsemann, E   1968.   *The testament of Jesus: A study of the gospel of John in the light of chapter 17.* London: SCM.

Kelber, W H   1976.   Conclusion: From Passion Narrative to gospel, in Kelber, W H (ed), *The passion in Mark: Studies in Mark 14-16* 153-180. Philadelphia: Fortress.

Kilpatrick, G D   1983.   *The eucharist in bible and liturgy.* Cambridge: Cambridge University Press.

Klos, H   1970.   *Die Sakramente im Johannesevangelium: Vorkommen und Bedeutung von Taufe, Eucharistie und Busse im vierten Evangelium.* Stuttgart: Katholisches Bibelwerk (SB 46).

Küng, H   [1976] 1978.   *On being a Christian.* London: Collins.

Kysar, R   1975.   *The fourth evangelist and his gospel.* Minneapolis: Augsburg.

Kysar, R   1977.   Community and gospel: Vectors in fourth gospel criticism. *Int* 31, 355-366.

Lampe, G H W (ed)   1961.   *A patristic Greek lexicon.* Oxford: Clarendon Press.

Leach, E   1983a.   Approaches to the study of the Bible, in Leach, E & Aycock, D A *Structuralist interpretations of biblical myth.* Cambridge: Cambridge University Press, 7-32.

Leach, E   1983b.   Against genres: are parables lights set in candlesticks or put under a bushel? in Leach, E & Aycock, D A *Structuralist interpretations of biblical myth.* Cambridge: Cambridge University Press, 89-112.

Lightfoot, R H   [1956] 1960.   *St John's gospel: A commentary.* C F Evans (ed). Oxford: Oxford University Press.

Lindars, B   1970.   Two parables in John. *NTS* 16, 318-329.

Lindars, B   1972.   *The gospel of John.* London: Oliphants (New Century Bible).

Lohse, B (hrsg)   1958.   *Die Passa-Homilie des bischofs Meliton von Sardis.* Leiden: Brill (Textus Minores 24).

Lohse, E   1961.   Wort und Sakrament im Johannesevangelium. *NTS* 7, 110-125.

Loisy, A   1921.   *Le quatrième évangile: Les épîtres dites de Jean.* ed 2. Paris: Nourry.

Louw, J P   1967.   Die semantiese waarde van die perfektum in Hellenistiese Grieks. *Acta Classica* 10, 23-32.

Lyonnet, S   1974.   La nature du culte chrétien: culte eucharistique et promulgation du "commandement nouveau". *Stud Miss* 23, 213-247.

McAllister, P A   1981.   *Umsindleko: A Gcaleka ritual of incorporation.* Grahamstown: Rhodes University (ISER occasional paper 26).

MacGregor, G H C   1963.   The eucharist in the fourth gospel. *NTS* 9, 111-119.

MacMullen, R   1967.   *Enemies of the Roman order: Treason, unrest and alienation in the Empire.* Cambridge, Massachusetts: Harvard University Press.

MacMullen, R   1981.   *Paganism in the Roman Empire.* New Haven: Yale University Press.

176   Works cited

Malatesta, E   1971.   The literary structure of John 17. *Biblica* 52, 190-214.

Malatesta, E   1977.   Blood and water from the pierced side of Christ (Jn 19,34), in Tragan 1977, 165-181.

Manns, F   1985.   Exégèse rabbinique et exégèse Johannique. *RB* 92, 525-538.

Marsh, J   1968.   *Saint John.* Harmondsworth: Penguin.

Marshall, I H   1978.   *The gospel of Luke.* Exeter: Paternoster.

Martyn, J L   1968.   *History and theology in the fourth gospel.* New York: Harper & Row.

Meeks, W A   1986.   The man from heaven in Johannine sectarianism, in Ashton, J (ed) *The interpretation of John,* 141-173. Philadelphia: Fortress (Issues in Religion & Theology 9).

Minear, P S   1977.   The audience of the fourth evangelist. *Int* 31, 339-354.

Moloney, F J   1975.   John 6 and the celebration of the eucharist. *Downside Review* 93, 243-251.

Morris, L   1964.   *The New Testament and Jewish lectionaries.* London: Tyndale.

Moule, C F D   1956.   The nature and purpose of I Peter. *NTS* 3, 1-11.

Moulton, J H & Milligan, G   1914-1929.   *The vocabulary of the Greek Testament illustrated from papyri and other sources.* London: Hodder & Stoughton.

Neill, S   1968.   *The church and Christian union.* London: Oxford University Press (Bampton lectures for 1964).

Niewalda, P   1958.   *Sacramentssymbolik im Johannesevangelium? Eine exegetisch-historische Studie.* Limburg: Lahn.

Nineham, D   [1976] 1978.   *The use and abuse of the bible: A study of the bible in an age of rapid cultural change.* London. SPCK.

Odeberg, H   [1929] 1974.   *The fourth gospel interpreted in its relation to contemporaneous religious currents in Palestine and the Hellenistic-Oriental world.* Reprint. Amsterdam: Gruener.

Painter, J   1979.   Johannine symbols: A case study in epistemology. *JThSA* 27, 26-41.

Pannenberg, W   1984.   *Christian spirituality and sacramental community.* London: DLT.

Paschal, R W Jr   1981.   Sacramental symbolism and physical imagery in the gospel of John. *Tyndale Bulletin* 32, 151-176.

Perrin, N   1976.   *Jesus and the language of the kingdom.* London: SCM.

Pierce, E L   1960.   The fourth gospel as drama. *Religion in Life* 29, 453-454.

Preuschen, E (hrsg)   1903.   *Origenes werke IV: Der Johanneskommentar.* Leipzig: Hinrichs (GCS).

Prickett, S   [1986] 1988.   *Words and the Word: Language, poetics and biblical interpretation.* Cambridge: Cambridge University Press.

Quispel, G   1970.   Love thy brother. *Ancient Society* 6, 83-93.

Robinson, J A T   1976.   *Redating the New Testament.* London: SCM.

Robinson, J A T   1985.   *The priority of John.* London: SCM.

Ruddick, C T   1968.   Feeding and sacrifice:the Old Testament background of the fourth gospel. *ExpT* 79, 340-341.

Sanders, E P   1977.   *Paul and Palestinian Judaism.* London: SCM.

Sandvik, B   1967.   Joh.15 als Abendmahlstext. *TZ* 23, 323-328.

Schillebeeckx, E   1963.   *Christ the sacrament of encounter with God.* London: Sheed & Ward.

Schnackenburg, R   1968.   *The gospel according to St John.* Vol 1 *Introduction and commentary on chapters 1-4.* London: Burns & Oates.

Schnackenburg, R   1982.   *The gospel according to St John.* Vol 3 *Commentary on chapters 13-21.* London: Burns & Oates.

Schneider, J   1951.   Zur Frage der Komposition von John 6, 27-58 (59), in Schmauch, W (hrsg) *In memoriam Ernst Lohmeyer,* 132-142. Stuttgart: Evang Verlagswerk.

Schneiders, S M   1977.   Symbolism and the sacramental principle in the fourth gospel, in Tragan 1977, 221-235.

Schweitzer, E   1959.   The concept of the church in the gospels and epistles of St John, in Higgins, A J B (ed) *New Testament essays: Studies in memory of Thomas Walter Manson 1893-1958,* 230-245. Manchester: Manchester University Press.

Schweizer, A   1931.   *The mysticism of Paul the apostle.* London: Black.

Shaw, A   1974.   The breakfast by the shore and the Mary Magdalene encounter as eucharistic narratives. *JThS* ns 25, 12-26.

Shaw, A   1975.   Image and symbol in John 21. *ExpT* 86, 311.

Smalley, S S   1978.   *John: Evangelist and interpreter.* Exeter: Paternoster.

Smith, M   [1973] 1982.   *The secret gospel: The discovery and interpretation of the secret gospel according to Mark.* Clearlake: Dawn Horse Press.

Steinbeck, J   [1939] 1966.   *The grapes of wrath.* London: Heinemann.

Suggit, J N   1981.   Nicodemus – the true Jew. *Neotestamentica* 14, 90-110.

Suggit, J N   1984.   John XVII.17 *JThS* ns 35, 104-117.

Talley, T J   1976.   From *berakah* to *eucharistia*: A reopening question. *Worship* 50, 115-137.

Thüsing, W   1970.   *Die Erhöhung und Verherrlichung Jesu im Johannesevangelium.* 2 Aufl. Munster: Aschendorff (NT Abhandlungen 21).

Thurian, M   1960/61.   *The eucharistic memorial.* 2 vols. Richmond: John Knox Press (Ecumenical Studies in Worship 7 & 8).

Thurian, M & Wainwright, G (eds)   1983.   *Baptism and eucharist: Ecumenical convergence in celebration.* Geneva: WCC (Faith and Order paper 117).

Tragan, P-R (ed)   1977.   *Segni e sacramenti nel vangelo di Giovanni.* Roma: Ed Anselmiana (Studia Anselmiana 66).

Tripp, D H   1981.   *Eperotema* (1 Peter 3:21): a liturgist's note. *ExpT* 92, 267-270.

Trocmé, E   1975.   *The formation of the gospel according to Mark.* London: SPCK.

Trocmé, E   1983.   *The Passion as liturgy : A study of the origin of the Passion Narratives in the four gospels.* London: SCM.

Vawter, B   1956.   The Johannine sacramentary. *ThS* 17, 151-166.

Venetz, H-J   1976.   Zeuge des Erhöten: Ein exegetischer Beitrag zu Joh 19,31-37. *Freiburger Zeitschrift für Philosophie und Theologie* 23, 81-111.

Vermes, G   1987.   *The Dead Sea scrolls in English.* 3rd ed. Harmondsworth: Penguin.

Von Allmen, J-J   1969.   *The Lord's Supper.* London: Lutterworth (Ecumenical Studies in Worship 19).

Wakefield, G S   1985.   *The Liturgy of St John.* Epworth.

Walker, W O   1982.   The Lord's Prayer in Matthew and John. *NTS* 28, 237-256.

Westcott, B F   1908.   *The gospel according to St John.* London: Murray.

World Council of Churches   1982.   *Baptism, eucharist and ministry.* Geneva: WCC (Faith and Order paper 111).

Wright, T R   1988.   *Theology and literature.* Oxford: Blackwell.

Indices